AMERICAN ILLUSTRATION 4

AMERICAN ILLUSTRATION
4

The fourth annual of American editorial, book, advertising, poster, promotional art, unpublished work, and film animation.

EDITED BY
EDWARD BOOTH-CLIBBORN

American Illustration, Inc. 67 Irving Place New York, New York 10003

Cover Illustration: Gene Greif
Book Design: Paula Scher/Tony Sellari
Design Assistant: Debra Bishop

Managing Editor: Lita Talarico
Assistant Editor: Marilyn Recht

Captions and artwork in this book have been supplied by the entrants.
While every effort has been made to ensure accuracy, American Illustration, Inc.
does not under any circumstances accept any responsibility for errors or
omissions.

If you are a practicing illustrator, artist, or student and would like to
submit work to the next annual competition write to:
American Illustration, Inc.
67 Irving Place
New York, New York 10003
(212) 460-5558

American Illustration, Inc. Call for Entries © copyright 1985

Distributed in the United States of America and Canada by:
Harry N. Abrams, Inc.
100 Fifth Avenue
New York, New York 10011
ISBN 0-8109-1829-3

France book distribution:
Editions Booth-Clibborn
Sofédis
29 rue St. Sulpice
75006 Paris, France

Book trade in the United Kingdom by:
Columbus Books
24 Elmfield Road
Bromley Kent, England

Book trade inquiries for the rest of the world:
Fleet Books
100 Park Avenue
New York, New York 10017

Direct mail, world:
Internos Books
Colville Road
London W38BL

Direct mail U.S.A., Canada:
Print Books
6400 Goldsboro Road
Bethesda, MD 20817

Printed and bound in Japan by Toppan Printing Company

Paper: 86 LB.(128gsm) TOP COAT/Kanzaki
Display Type: Wood Type from Koppel & Scher
Text Type: Bodoni Book
Typesetting and Mechanicals: 7 Graphic Arts/Koppel & Scher

CONTENTS

INTRODUCTION

Edward Booth-Clibborn

What price originality?

In the illustrator's world, originality is an elusive quality, sought after as some might search for gold in the seams of an over-worked mining shaft.

Happily, originality is here in abundance in this fourth edition of *AMERICAN ILLUSTRATION*.

What makes for originality? And what price does it exact?

For my part, I believe it to be the almost divine conjunction of the gift of drawing and the craft of work—Thomas Edison's "five per cent inspiration, ninety-five per cent perspiration."

Of course, it takes time to develop.

It begins—or should begin—when aspiring illustrators are starting art school. It relies on the student's nerve; the ability to see that drawing is a way of seeing and that the pencil is an extension of the self.

When I talk to my students I always lay this ground rule before we go any further. I tell them to keep an "ideas book" or a sketch book. For it's in such a book that the illustrator will only find himself, or herself, and where originality, if it is to be found, will develop.

Wherever the artist is, what he or she sees, and draws, provides the means to discover his or her own originality. And of course, the sketchbook endures: what they have seen and drawn will stay with them forever, a reminder of how they saw what they saw, at that time, and how they responded to it.

This is particularly valuable in the event of visits to foreign countries or new places. Such trips always heighten the senses. They are like an awakening, or a rebirth, from the familiar or mundane. At times like this the illustrator's self is at its most exposed. The mind's eye has a more piercing vision. The very shock of the differentness makes the self react to the surroundings in an almost startlingly unique way.

The sketches should record this, at every step.

Little drawings of everything that catches the eye. Sketched responses to sounds and smells. Not works of art but explorations along the track of the internal voyage of discovery.

This is where originality begins and, in my view, where it should be kept, at least until the illustrator's position is assured and his or her reputation established. It's an awful twentieth century concept that illustrators' sketch books should be counted as works of art. Books of work is what they are; books of work is how they should be seen.

And at the heart of all this lies the craft of drawing.

Some years ago now, art schools began to move away from the idea of learning the fundamentals, placing much more emphasis on the art of seeing. Unfortunately, what you have seen—or even what you have dreamed up—cannot be seen by others unless you have command of the language of communication. So just as a writer must command grammar, or a musician understand the ground rules of composition, so must the illustrator have a firm grip on the principles of good drawing.

In the pages of this book you will see the result of some of the most assiduous years of working at drawing. Some of these works may give the impression of easiness, as if dashed off in a moment or two with no effort or thought. Do not be misled. None of the work here has come easy; none of it is slight or trivial. Each has well and truly earned its place in these pages.

This is as true of the work of seasoned professionals as it is of the work of young students, all of whose submissions we judge on an equal basis.

To sum up: originality, which brings acclaim, is the result of a spark of genius allied to the fuel of work.

THE JURY

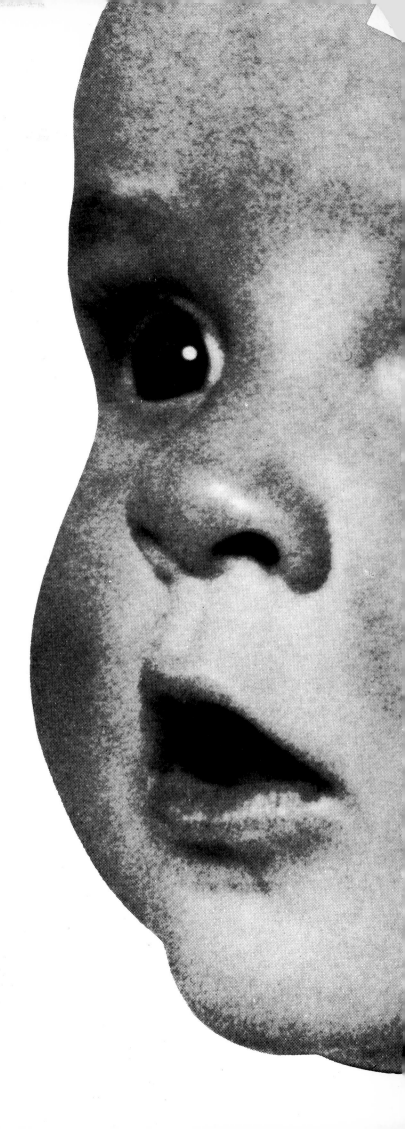

PAUL HARDY

Paul Hardy has been Senior Designer and Art Director for Hinrichs Design Associates as well as founding Art Director of *Working Woman* and *Attenzione* magazines. In 1981 he formed Paul Hardy Design Associates with Miles Abernethy. His redesign projects include *Family Circle, Money, Interiors, The Baltimore Sun*, and other magazines and supplements. He has received awards from the Art Director's Club, AIGA, The Society of Illustrators (Gold Medal), CA, The Andy Awards, and others.

JERRY HERRING

Jerry Herring formed Herring Design in 1973. The studio produces brochures, annual reports, marketing materials, editorial design and trademarks for institutions and corporations. The desire to publish his book project designs led to the formation of Herring Press and Graphic Design Press in 1984. The first of these projects are *Historic Galveston* and *100 Texas Posters*. He is former president of the Art Director's Club of Houston and current president of the American Institute of Graphic Arts, Texas Chapter.

KIT HINRICHS

Kit Hinrichs worked as a designer in several New York design offices before forming the design team that would eventually be Jonson Pedersen Hinrichs & Shakery. His work incorporates a wide range of projects including annual reports, sales promotions, exhibits, and editorial graphics.

TERRY O'MALLEY

Terry O'Malley is Executive Creative Director of Vickers & Benson, where he has worked for the past 22 years. His accounts include Ford, Gulf, Bank of Montreal, Toronto Star, Hiram Walker and many others. He also devotes a great deal of time to public service works such as Canadian Save the Children, Pollution Probe, Multiple Sclerosis, The United Way, the United Jewish Appeal, and more. He has received over 100 awards in all media.

APRIL SILVER

April Silver began her career with *Esquire* magazine in 1979 as an Associate Art Director, and in 1983 was promoted to Art Director. Prior to that she worked at *Rolling Stone* magazine. She is a winner of numerous national and international design awards, a member of various juries and was recently invited to speak in the "Creative Design" lecture series at the Smithsonian Institute.

EDITORIAL

This section includes illustrations for newspapers and their
supplements, consumer, trade and tenhnical magazines, and
periodicals.

19 ARTIST/DESIGNER
    ANTHONY PACK

ART DIRECTOR
CHRISTINA JEPSEN

PUBLICATION
KANSAS ALUMNI MAGAZINE

PUBLISHER
ALUMNI ASSOCIATION OF THE UNIVERSITY OF KANSAS

WRITER
EDGAR WOLFE

Illustration for a story entitled "A Creature Most Gentle," January 1985.

Acrylic

20 ARTIST
GUY BILLOUT

DESIGNER/ART DIRECTOR
JUDY GARLAN

PUBLICATION
THE ATLANTIC

PUBLISHER
THE ATLANTIC MONTHLY CO.

"Perfectionism," one in a series of full-page
paintings by the artist, April 1984.

Watercolor

21 ARTIST
GUY BILLOUT

DESIGNER/ART DIRECTOR
JUDY GARLAN

PUBLICATION
THE ATLANTIC

PUBLISHER
THE ATLANTIC MONTHLY CO.

"Drought," one in a series of full-page
paintings by the artist, December 1984.

Watercolor

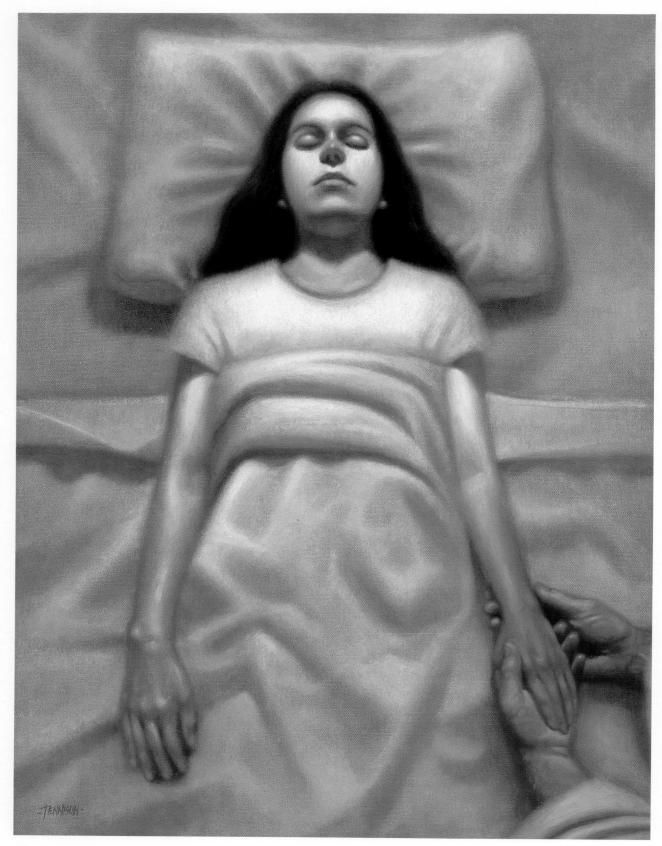

22 ARTIST
JAMES E. TENNISON

ART DIRECTOR
HILBER NELSON

PUBLICATION
DISCIPLESHIP JOURNAL

PUBLISHER
THE NAVIGATORS

WRITER
REV. JOHN H. STEVENS

Illustration for an article entitled "His Life—
Giving Touch," December 1984.

Oil on canvas

23 ARTIST
TOM CURRY

DESIGNER
HILBER NELSON

ART DIRECTORS
TOM CURRY/HILBER NELSON

PUBLICATION
DISCIPLESHIP JOURNAL

PUBLISHER
THE NAVIGATORS

WRITER
STEVE TROXEL

Illustration for an article entitled "Taming
Your Feelings," March 1, 1985.

Acrylic

24 ARTIST
ALEXA GRACE

DESIGNER/ART DIRECTOR
RONN CAMPISI

PUBLICATION
THE BOSTON GLOBE MAGAZINE

PUBLISHER
AFFILIATED PUBLICATIONS

WRITER
FANNY HOWE

Illustration for a story entitled "Elevator,"
May 20, 1984.

Pastel, ink, and watercolor

25 ARTIST
ALEXA GRACE

ART DIRECTOR
CHRISTOPHER AUSTOPCHUK

PUBLICATION
SELF

PUBLISHER
CONDÉ NAST PUBLICATIONS

WRITER
SARAH E. LANG

Illustration for an article entitled "The New Patchwork Families," June 1984.

Watercolor and pastel

26 ARTIST
KINUKO Y. CRAFT

ART DIRECTOR
MICHAEL GROSSMAN

PUBLICATION
NATIONAL LAMPOON

PUBLISHER
NL COMMUNICATIONS, INC.

Illustration for an article entitled "Alleluia,"
May 1984.

Egg tempera and gold leaf

27 ARTIST
ROBERT GIUSTI

ART DIRECTOR
THEO KOUVATSOS

PUBLICATION
PLAYBOY

PUBLISHER
PLAYBOY ENTERPRISES, INC.

WRITER
WILLIAM F. BUCKLEY, JR.

Illustration for an article entitled
"Redefining Smart," January 1985.

Acrylic on masonite

28 ARTIST
GENE GREIF

ART DIRECTOR
JAY PURVIS

PUBLICATION
GENTLEMAN'S QUARTERLY

PUBLISHER
CONDÉ NAST PUBLICATIONS

WRITER
SAM KEEN

Illustration for an article entitled "Male
Friendship: A Guilt-Edged Bond," May 1984.

Collage

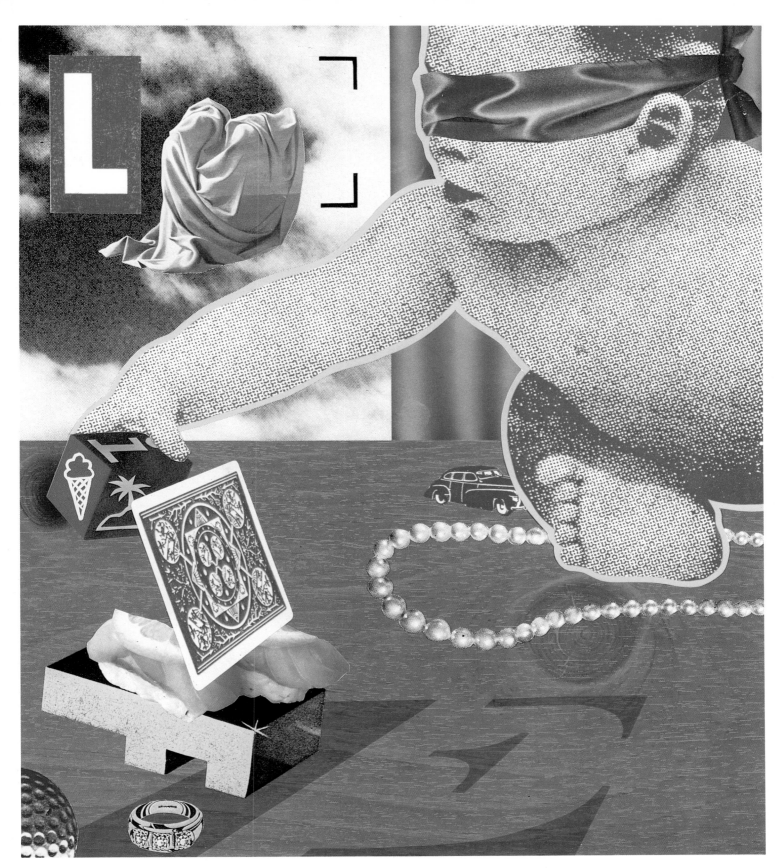

29 ARTIST
GENE GREIF

ART DIRECTOR
RONN CAMPISI

PUBLICATION
THE BOSTON GLOBE MAGAZINE

PUBLISHER
AFFILIATED PUBLICATIONS

WRITER
EMILY HIESTAND

Illustration for an article about the word
'lifestyle' entitled "May I Have a Word With
You," February 24, 1985.

Collage

30 ARTIST
DOUG SMITH

DESIGNER
MARK ULRICH

ART EDITOR
PETER DEUTSCH

PUBLICATION
AT&T MAGAZINE

WRITER
ROBERT M. KAUNER

Illustration for an article entitled
"A Corporate Match Point," August 1984.

Scratchboard and watercolor

31 ARTIST
DOUG SMITH

DESIGNER/ART DIRECTOR
HANS TEENSMA

PUBLICATION
NEW ENGLAND MONTHLY

PUBLISHER
NEW ENGLAND MONTHLY, INC.

WRITER
JOHN N. COLE

Illustration for an article
"The Electric Ocean," May 1984.

Scratchboard and watercolor

32 ARTIST
ANITA KUNZ

DESIGNER/ART EDITOR
JOHN TWOHEY

PUBLICATION
CHICAGO TRIBUNE

PUBLISHER
THE CHICAGO TRIBUNE CO.

Illustration for an article entitled "Seductive
Fragrances," April 8, 1984.

Watercolor and gouache

33   ARTIST
ANITA KUNZ

DESIGNER/ART DIRECTOR
GILVRIE MISSTEAR

PUBLICATION
THE SUNDAY TIMES MAGAZINE, LONDON

PUBLISHER
THE SUNDAY TIMES

Illustration for an article entitled "Behaviour/
Battle of the Binge," September 1984.

Watercolor and gouache

34 ARTIST
BLAIR DRAWSON

DESIGNER
JUDY GOLDSTEIN

ART DIRECTOR
APRIL SILVER

PUBLICATION
ESQUIRE

PUBLISHER
ESQUIRE ASSOCIATES INC.

WRITER
C.D.B. BRYAN

Illustrations for an article entitled "Sex and the Married Man," June 1984.

Gouache and watercolor

36 ARTIST
MARK PENBERTHY

DESIGNER/ART DIRECTOR
KEN KENDRICK

PUBLICATION
NEW YORK TIMES MAGAZINE

PUBLISHER
THE NEW YORK TIMES

WRITER
MARK KRAMER

Illustration for an article entitled "Waiting for
Next Time" on the "About Men" page,
December 16, 1984.

Oil

37 ARTIST
MARK PENBERTHY

CREATIVE DIRECTOR
PETER J. BLANK

ART DIRECTOR
MARY ZISK

PUBLICATION
PC MAGAZINE

PUBLISHER
ZIFF-DAVIS PUBLISHING CO.

WRITERS
DIANE BURNS/S. VENIT

Illustration for an article entitled "Enable
Does it Right," February 19, 1985.

Oil

38 ARTIST
PHILIPPE WEISBECKER

DESIGNER
MARK ULRICH

ART DIRECTOR
ANTHONY RUSSELL

PUBLICATION
MHC TODAY

WRITER
JOHN STEFANS

Illustration for an article entitled
"On the Ground and Running Where the
Action Is," Annual Report 1984.

Ink and watercolor

39 ARTIST
PHILIPPE WEISBECKER

DESIGNER
MARK ULRICH

ART DIRECTOR
PETER DEUTSCH

PUBLICATION
AT&T MAGAZINE

WRITER
LEN MORAN

Illustration for an article about the AT&T
divestiture entitled "Setting Sail With One
Enterprise, One Mission, One Measure,"
April 1984.

Ink and watercolor

40 ARTIST
MELISSA GRIMES

DESIGNER/ART DIRECTOR
FRED WOODWARD

PUBLICATION
TEXAS MONTHLY

PUBLISHER
TEXAS MONTHLY, INC.

"Bluebonnet Picture," for a feature entitled
"Western Art," November 1984.

Collage

41   ARTIST
MELISSA GRIMES

DESIGNER/ART DIRECTOR
BILL HEWSON

PUBLICATION
THE TEXAS HUMANIST

PUBLISHER
TEXAS COMMISSION FOR THE HUMANITIES

WRITER
ERIC MUIRHEAD

Illustration for an article about American oil-
rig workers in Malaysia entitled "Kinabalu
and the Roughneck," March/April 1984.

Collage

42 ARTIST
JOHN COLLIER

ART DIRECTOR
TINA ADAMEK

PUBLICATION
POSTGRADUATE MEDICINE

PUBLISHER
McGRAW-HILL PUBLISHING

WRITER
JACK L. CLARK

Illustration for an article entitled
"Overview of Face Pain," August 1984.

Oil

43 ARTIST
BRUCE WOLFE

ART DIRECTOR
KERIG POPE

PUBLICATION
PLAYBOY

PUBLISHER
PLAYBOY ENTERPRISES, INC.

WRITER
JOHN GARDINER

Illustration for a story entitled "Julius Caesar
and Werewolf," September 1984.

Oil

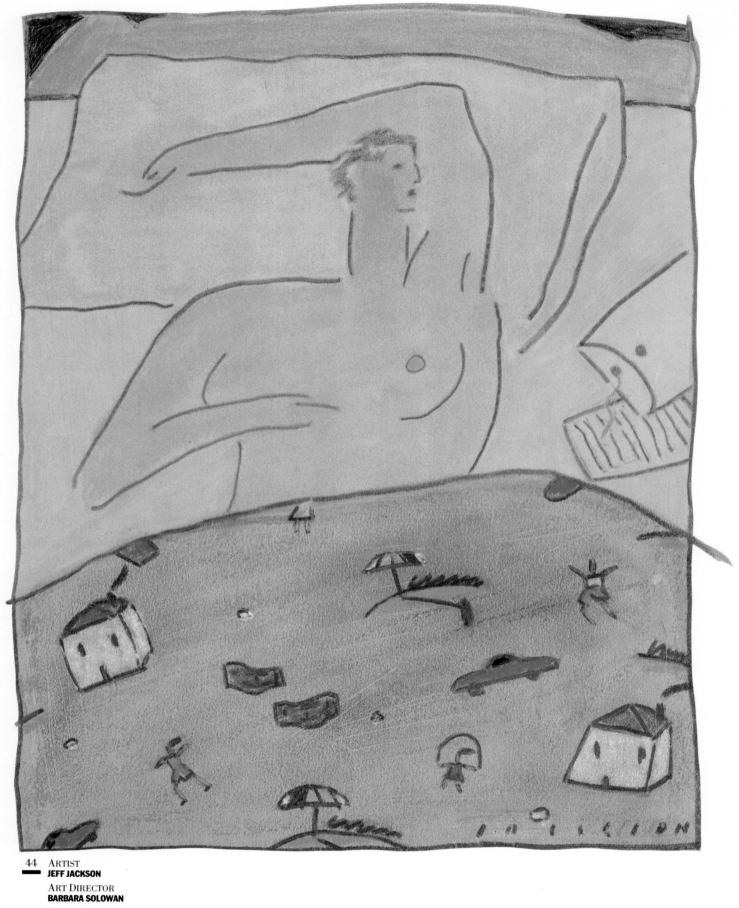

44 ARTIST
JEFF JACKSON

ART DIRECTOR
BARBARA SOLOWAN

PUBLICATION
CITY WOMAN MAGAZINE

PUBLISHER
COMAC COMMUNICATIONS LTD.

WRITER
BETTY LEE

Illustration for an article entitled "Rest Insured," 1984.

Chalk and gouache

45 ARTIST
BLAIR DRAWSON

ART DIRECTOR
PROSPER ASSOULINE

PUBLICATION
LA MODE EN PEINTURE

PUBLISHER
LA SOCIÉTÉ PROSPER

Illustration for an article entitled "Mode,"
(Fashion) April/May 1985.

Watercolor

46 ARTIST
BRAD HOLLAND

DESIGNER/ART EDITOR
JOHN TWOHEY

PUBLICATION
CHICAGO TRIBUNE

PUBLISHER
THE CHICAGO TRIBUNE CO.

WRITER
LEN ACKLAND

Cover illustration for an article on the nuclear
time bomb entitled "Sounding the Alarm,"
March 11, 1984.

Acrylic on canvas

47 ARTIST
BRAD HOLLAND

ART DIRECTORS
BOB ENGLE/RON MEYERSON

PUBLICATION
NEWSWEEK

PUBLISHER
NEWSWEEK, INC.

WRITER
JERRY ADLER

Cover illustration for an article entitled
"Phobias," April 23, 1984.

Acrylic on masonite

48 ARTIST
GUY BILLOUT

DESIGNER/ART DIRECTOR
JUDY GARLAN

PUBLICATION
THE ATLANTIC

PUBLISHER
THE ATLANTIC MONTHLY CO.

WRITER
DAVID DENBY

Cover illustration for a story entitled
"Theaterphobia," January 1985.

Watercolor

49 ARTIST
GUY BILLOUT

ART EDITOR
DOROTHY WICKENDEN

PUBLICATION
THE NEW REPUBLIC

PUBLISHER
THE NEW REPUBLIC

WRITER
JEAN BETHKE ELSHTAIN

Cover illustration for a story entitled
"Women, Politics, and Pornography," June
25, 1984.

Watercolor and airbrush

50 ARTIST
STEVE CARVER

ART DIRECTOR
MARTY BRAUN

PUBLICATION
THE BOSTON GLOBE MAGAZINE

PUBLISHER
AFFILIATED PUBLICATIONS

WRITER
DAVID WARSH

Illustration for an article entitled "Why Your
Dollar is Shrinking," August 19, 1984.

Acrylic and alkyd

51 ARTIST
MARCIA STIEGER

ART DIRECTOR
VERONIQUE VIENNE

PUBLICATION
CALIFORNIA LIVING MAGAZINE

PUBLISHER
SAN FRANCISCO EXAMINER

Illustrations for an article about a process of
creating miniature art, February 3, 1985.

Colored pencil on oriented polystyrene

52 ARTIST
GUY BILLOUT

DESIGNER/ART DIRECTOR
JUDY GARLAN

PUBLICATION
THE ATLANTIC

PUBLISHER
THE ATLANTIC MONTHLY CO.

"Persistence," one in a series of full-page
paintings by the artist, June 1984.

Watercolor

53 ARTIST
GUY BILLOUT

ART DIRECTOR
BARBARA KOSTER

PUBLICATION
TWA AMBASSADOR

PUBLISHER
PAULSEN PUBLISHING COMPANY

WRITER
BONNIE BLODGETT

"The Lonely Person's Garden," one of several
illustrations depicting imaginary gardens,
June 1984.

Watercolor

54 ARTIST
ANITA KUNZ

DESIGNER
JOLENE CUYLER

ART DIRECTOR
LOUIS FISHAUF

PUBLICATION
SATURDAY NIGHT

PUBLISHER
SATURDAY NIGHT PUBLISHING

WRITER
GEORGE WOODCOCK

Portrait for a memoir entitled "The Political Blacklisting of a Canadian Writer," August 1984.

Watercolor and gouache

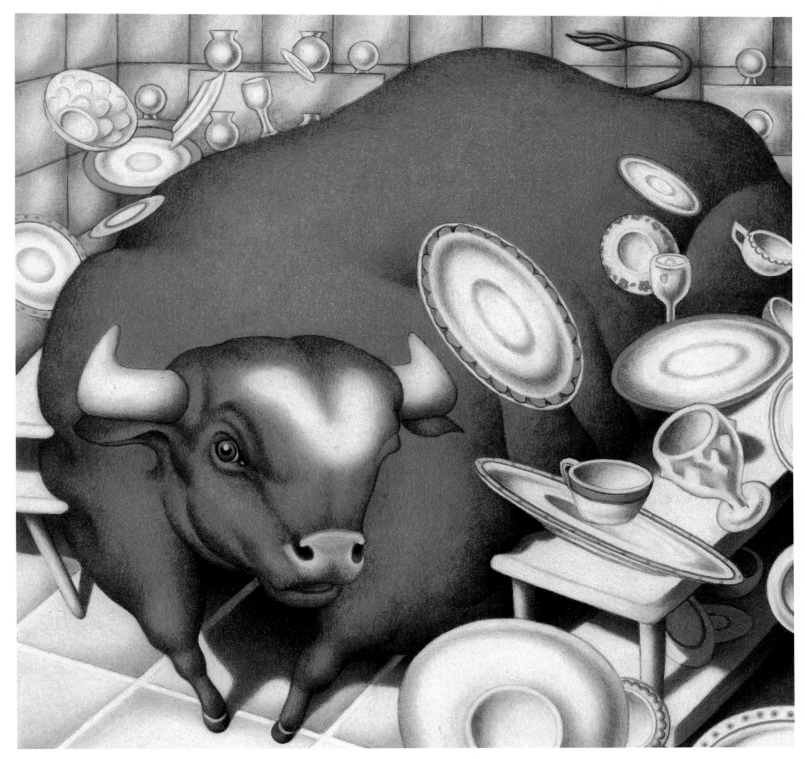

55 ARTIST
AMY HILL

ART DIRECTOR
ELLEN BLISSMAN

PUBLICATION
MONEY MAGAZINE

PUBLISHER
TIME INC.

WRITER
MARLYS HARRIS

Illustration for a story on Merrill Lynch
entitled "The Stumbling Herd,"
November 1984.

Colored pencil

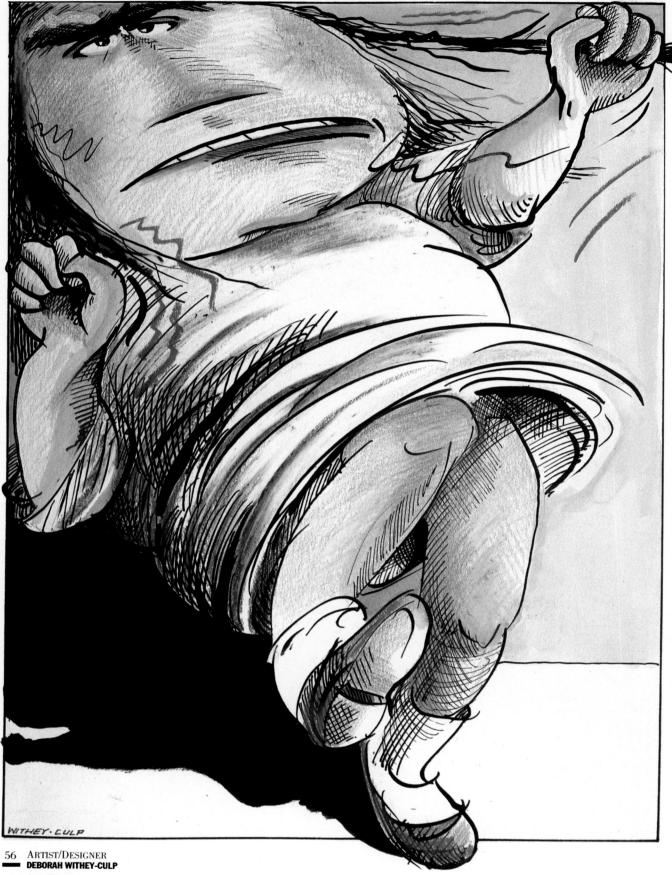

WITHEY·CULP

56 ARTIST/DESIGNER
DEBORAH WITHEY-CULP

ART DIRECTOR
BROC SEARS

PUBLICATION
DALLAS TIMES HERALD

PUBLISHER
DALLAS TIMES HERALD

WRITER
MARK ZUSSMAN

Illustration for an article entitled "Conquering
Your Frustrations," May 6, 1984.

India ink and water soluble crayon

57 ARTIST
GEOFFREY MOSS

DESIGNER
MARK ULRICH

ART EDITOR
PETER DEUTSCH

PUBLICATION
AT&T MAGAZINE

WRITER
CROCKER SNOW JR.

Illustration for an article entitled
"Beyond One's Nose," August 1984.

Litho pencil and watercolor

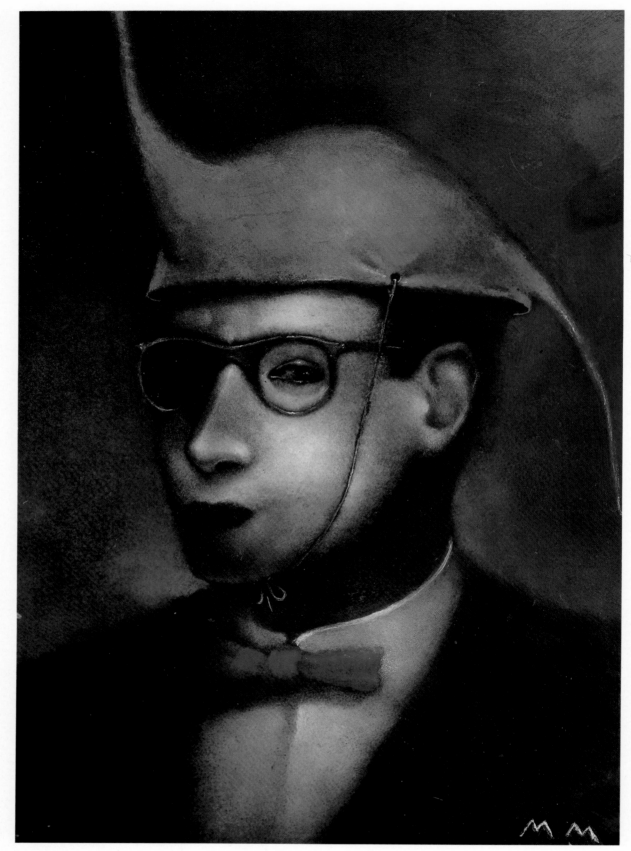

58 ARTIST
MATT MAHURIN

DESIGNER/ART DIRECTOR
HANS TEENSMA

PUBLICATION
NEW ENGLAND MONTHLY

PUBLISHER
NEW ENGLAND MONTHLY, INC.

WRITER
GEORGE V. HIGGINS

Ilustration for an article on the demise of the
Boston lawyer entitled "Tyrannosaurus Lex,"
1984.

Oil

59 ARTIST
MATT MAHURIN

DESIGNER
WAYNE FITZPATRICK

PUBLICATION
SCIENCE 84 MAGAZINE

PUBLISHER
**AMERICAN ASSOCIATION FOR THE ADVANCEMENT
OF SCIENCE**

WRITER
WILLIAM F. ALLMAN

Illustration for an article entitled "Nice Guys
Finish First," 1984.

Oil

60 ARTIST
JULIAN ALLEN

ART DIRECTOR
VERONIQUE VIENNE

PUBLICATION
WEST

PUBLISHER
SAN JOSE MERCURY NEWS

Illustration for an article entitled
"The Star of Stars," November 11, 1984.

Watercolor

61 ARTIST
CHRIS PAYNE

DESIGNERS
FRED WOODWARD/DAVID KAMPA

ART DIRECTOR
FRED WOODWARD

PUBLICATION
TEXAS MONTHLY

PUBLISHER
TEXAS MONTHLY, INC.

WRITER
WILLIAM J. HELMER

Illustration for a story entitled "Hub Cafe,"
April 1984.

Oil, pencil, gouache, and acrylic

62 ARTIST
HENRIK DRESCHER

DESIGNER
ERIC MURPHY

PUBLICATION
POPULAR COMPUTING

PUBLISHER
McGRAW-HILL PUBLISHING

WRITER
G. BERTON LATAMORE

Illustration for an article entitled "The
Business Connection," March 1985.

Watercolor and pen and ink

63 ARTIST
HENRIK DRESCHER

DESIGNER
ERIC MURPHY

PUBLICATION
POPULAR COMPUTING

PUBLISHER
McGRAW-HILL PUBLISHING

WRITER
LOUIS JAFFE

Illustration for an article entitled "Convenient
Conferences," March 1985.

Watercolor and pen and ink

64 ARTIST/ART DIRECTOR
STAN McCRAY

PUBLICATION
BOSTON MAGAZINE

WRITER
MARGERY EAGAN

Illustration for an article entitled
"Help, Police," April 1984.

Acrylic paint

65 ARTIST
KUNIYASU

DESIGNER
ELIZABETH WILLIAMS

ART DIRECTOR
DEREK UNGLESS

PUBLICATION
ROLLING STONE

PUBLISHER
STRAIGHT ARROW PUBLISHERS INC.

WRITER
CHRISTOPHER CONNELLY

Portrait of Annie Lennox for an article entitled
"Eurythmics and the Language of Love,"
February 2, 1984.

Pastel

66 ARTIST
STEVEN GUARNACCIA

DESIGNER/ART DIRECTOR
RONN CAMPISI

PUBLICATION
THE BOSTON GLOBE MAGAZINE

PUBLISHER
AFFILIATED PUBLICATIONS

WRITER
EMILY HIESTAND

Illustration for an article entitled
"The Compleat Shoveler," January 1, 1984.

Watercolor and pen and ink

67 ARTIST
STEVEN GUARNACCIA

ART DIRECTOR
RONN CAMPISI

PUBLICATION
THE BOSTON GLOBE MAGAZINE

PUBLISHER
AFFILIATED PUBLICATIONS

WRITER
SUSAN TRAUSCH

Illustration for an article about a Boston
journalist moving to Washington entitled "No
Laughing Matter," September 16, 1984.

Pen and ink and watercolor

68 ARTIST
RICHARD ROSS

DESIGNER/ART DIRECTOR
RIKI ALLRED

PUBLICATION
NORTHEAST MAGAZINE

PUBLISHER
THE HARTFORD COURANT

WRITER
RUTH DOAN MACDOUGALL

Illustration for a short story entitled
"Surprise," June 3, 1984.

Pastel

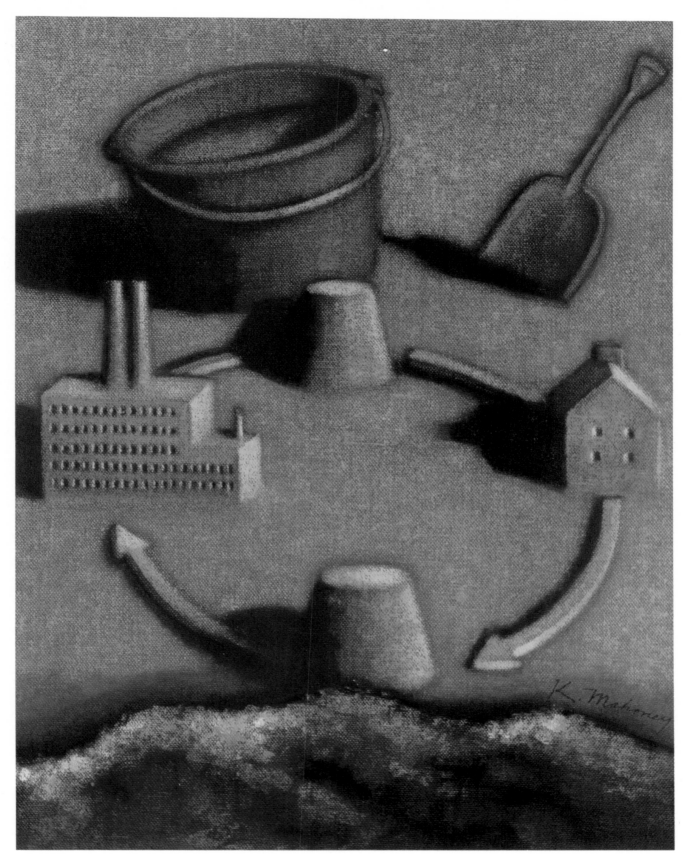

69 ARTIST
KATHERINE MAHONEY

ART DIRECTOR
SUSAN F. SHEPHERD

PUBLICATION
PURCHASING MAGAZINE

PUBLISHER
CAHNERS PUBLISHING

WRITER
J. WILLIAM SEMICH

Illustration for a story entitled
"The Keynesian Recovery in '85,"
November 29, 1984.

Oil

70 ARTIST
ELWYN MEHLMAN

DESIGNER/ART DIRECTOR
NICK DANKOVICH

PUBLICATION
INDUSTRY WEEK

PUBLISHER
PENTON/IPC

WRITER
B. CHARLES AMES

Illustration for an article entitled "Down-
Sizing Your Company," February 18, 1985.

Watercolor

71 ARTIST
ELWOOD H. SMITH

DESIGNER
DAN JURSA

ART EDITOR
JOHN TWOHEY

PUBLICATION
CHICAGO TRIBUNE SUNDAY MAGAZINE

PUBLISHER
THE CHICAGO TRIBUNE CO.

WRITER
MICHAEL HIRSLEY

Cover illustration for "The 1984 News-Is-
Stranger-Than-Fiction Scrapbook,"
December 30, 1984.

Watercolor and India ink

72 ARTIST/ART DIRECTOR
TED PITTS

PUBLICATION
THE MIAMI HERALD

PUBLISHER
THE MIAMI HERALD

WRITER
CHRISTOPHER BOYD

Illustration for an article entitled "A Bumper
Crop of Rentals," June 24, 1984.

Pencil, watercolor, and acrylic

73 ARTIST
STEVE CARVER

ART DIRECTOR
MARY SHANAHAN

PUBLICATION
CUISINE MAGAZINE

PUBLISHER
CBS MAGAZINES

WRITER
KAY SHAW NELSON

Illustration for an article entitled "Pitching in
Makes the Picnic," July 1984.

Acrylic and gouache

74 ARTIST
JEFF DODSON

ART DIRECTOR
GREG PAUL

PUBLICATION
SUNSHINE MAGAZINE

PUBLISHER
FT. LAUDERDALE NEWS & SUN SENTINEL

WRITER
JOHN ROTHCHILD

Illustration for an article entitled "Sin Cities,"
January 6, 1985.

Mixed media

75 ARTIST
MARSHALL ARISMAN

ART DIRECTOR
LESTER GOODMAN

PUBLICATION
PSYCHOLOGY TODAY

PUBLISHER
AMERICAN PSYCHOLOGICAL ASSOCIATION

WRITER
MARCIA YUDKIN

Illustration for an article entitled
"When Kids Think the Unthinkable,"
September 1984.

Oil on paper

76 ARTIST
VAL FRASER

ART DIRECTOR
BARBARA SOLOWAN

PUBLICATION
CITY WOMAN MAGAZINE

PUBLISHER
COMAC COMMUNICATIONS LTD.

Illustration for an article entitled "Don't Be
Helpless About Stress," Fall 1984.

Collage with airbrush

77 ARTIST
SHEBA ROSS

DESIGNER
CHARLES BRUCALIERE

ART DIRECTOR
APRIL SILVER

PUBLICATION
ESQUIRE

PUBLISHER
ESQUIRE ASSOCIATES INC.

WRITER
RON ROSENBAUM

Illustration for an article entitled "The
Chemistry of Love," June 1984.

Acrylic

78 ARTIST
MATT MAHURIN

DESIGNER
ANDY KNER

PUBLICATION
PRINT MAGAZINE

WRITER
STEVEN HELLER

Illustration for an article on the artist entitled
"Young Artist With a Dark Vision,"
May/June 1984.

Oil

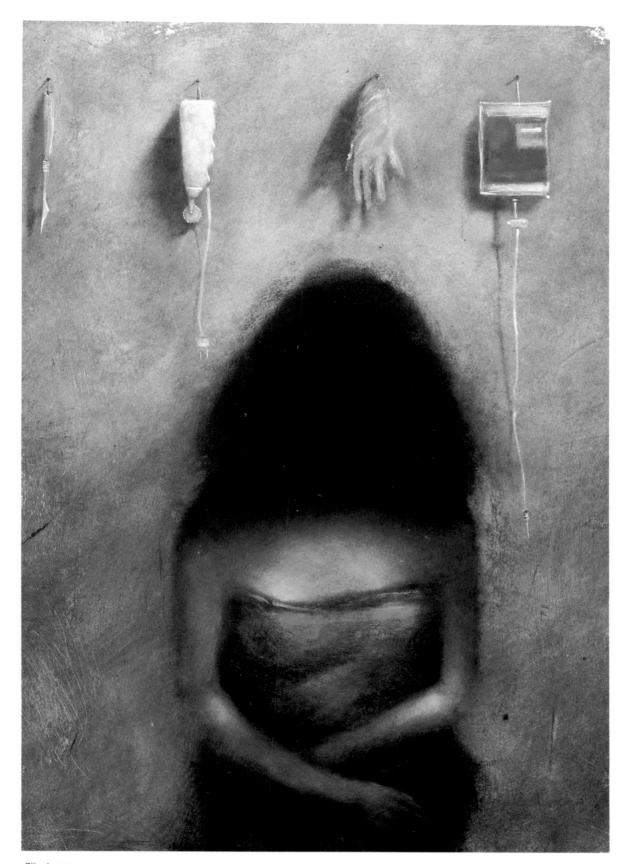

79 ARTIST
MATT MAHURIN

DESIGNER
JUDY GOLDSTEIN

ART DIRECTOR
MICHAEL VALENTI

PUBLICATION
SCIENCE DIGEST

PUBLISHER
HEARST CORPORATION

WRITER
RICHARD SEVERO

Illustration for an article entitled "Annals of
Surgery," February 1985.

Acrylic

80 ARTIST
JULIE EVANS

ART DIRECTOR
MEG RICHICHI

PUBLICATION
DIABETES FORECAST

PUBLISHER
AMERICAN DIABETES ASSOCIATION

WRITERS
BARBARA J. ANDERSON/HELEN KORNBLUM

Illustration for an article entitled "What's
With That Kid," September/October 1984.

Acrylic

81 ARTIST
SEYMOUR CHWAST

ART DIRECTOR
HANS-GEORG POSPISCHIL

PUBLICATION
FRANKFURTER ALLGEMEINE MAGAZIN

PUBLISHER
FRANKFURTER ALLGEMEINE ZEITUNG GmbH.

Illustration for a story on computers, March 1984.

Cello-tak and rapidograph

82 ARTIST
— **BARRY ROOT**

ART DIRECTOR
KEN KENDRICK

PUBLICATION
NEW YORK TIMES MAGAZINE

PUBLISHER
THE NEW YORK TIMES

WRITER
STEVE TESSICH

Illustration for an article entitled
"An Amateur Marriage," September 1984.

Watercolor and gouache

83 ARTIST
MARY LYNN BLASUTTA

DESIGNER
CASEY CLARK

ART DIRECTOR
ANTHONY RUSSELL

PUBLICATION
FINANCIAL ENTERPRISE

PUBLISHER
GENERAL ELECTRIC CREDIT CORP.

Illustration for an article entitled "Decade of
the Entrepreneur," Spring 1985.

Watercolor

84 ARTIST
LOU BROOKS

DESIGNERS
DAVID BAYER/LOU BROOKS

ART DIRECTORS
MICHAEL VALENTI/DAVID BAYER

PUBLICATION
SCIENCE DIGEST

PUBLISHER
HEARST CORPORATION

WRITER
DR. CRYPTON

Illustration for a feature entiled "Dr.
Crypton's Great Hoax Contest," February
1985.

Pen and ink, airbrush, and color overlays

85 ARTIST/DESIGNER
EARL KELENY

ART DIRECTOR
ALICE DEGENHARDT

PUBLICATION
CREATIVE LIVING MAGAZINE

PUBLISHER
NORTHWESTERN MUTUAL LIFE

WRITER
NEIL CLARK WARREN

Illustration for an article entitled "Taming the
Anger Demon," Winter/Spring 1984.

Acrylic and prismacolor

86 Artist
REGAN DUNNICK

Designer/Art Director
JAMES NOEL SMITH

Publication
WESTWARD

Publisher
DALLAS TIMES HERALD

Writer
JAMES WAKEFIELD BURKE

Illustration for an article entitled
"David Crockett—The Man Behind the
Myth," December 2, 1984.

Pastel

87 ARTIST
REGAN DUNNICK

DESIGNER/ART DIRECTOR
JEFF STANTON

PUBLICATION
D MAGAZINE

PUBLISHER
SOUTHWEST MEDIA CORP.

WRITER
JO BRANS

Illustration for an article entitled
"Manhattan Transfer." February 1985.

Pastel

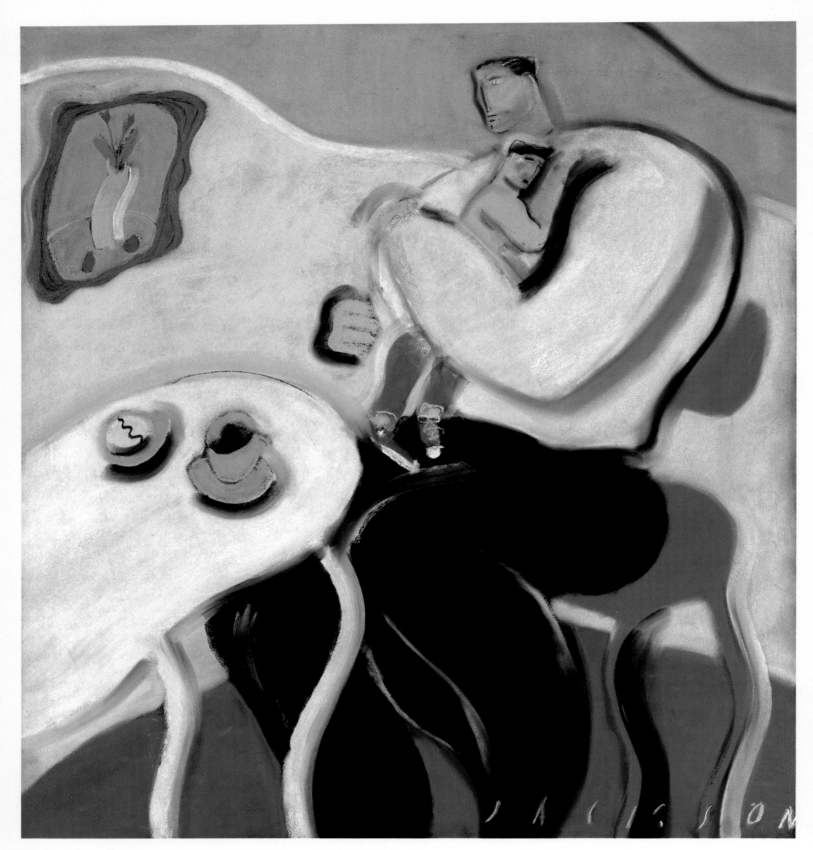

88 ARTIST
JEFF JACKSON

DESIGNER
JOLENE CUYLER

ART DIRECTOR
LOUIS FISHAUF

PUBLICATION
SATURDAY NIGHT

PUBLISHER
SATURDAY NIGHT PUBLISHING

WRITER
ROBIN MATHEWS

Illustration for a fiction piece entitled "His Own Son," January 1984.

Pastel

89 ARTIST
PAOLA PIGLIA

DESIGNER
NORA SHEEHAN

ART DIRECTOR
BOB CIANO

PUBLICATION
LIFE

PUBLISHER
TIME-LIFE INC.

Illustration for a feature entitled "Voices: Money Talks," January 1985.

Mixed Media

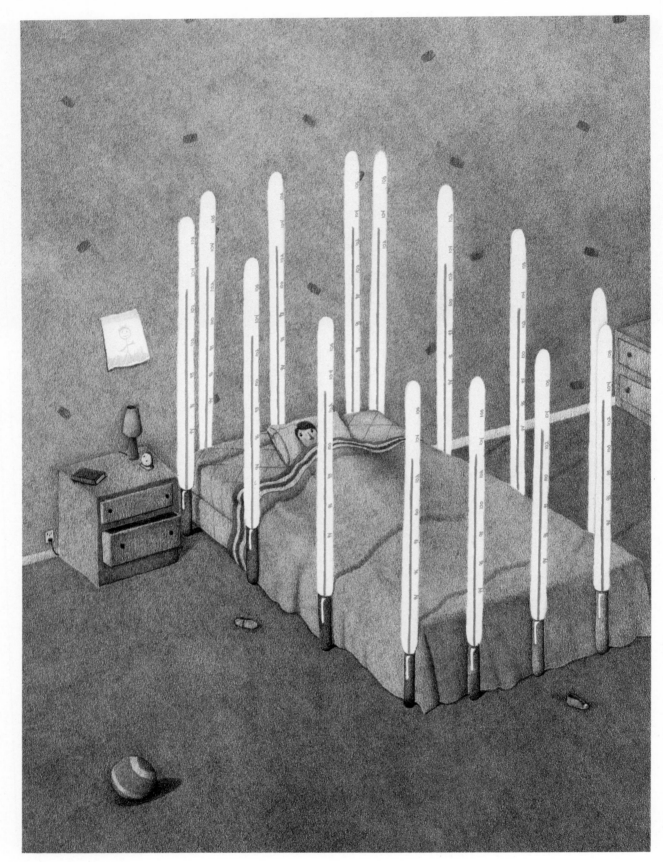

90 ARTIST
PAUL YALOWITZ

ART DIRECTOR
JAMES WALSH

PUBLICATION
EMERGENCY MEDICINE

WRITER
MICHAEL LEVI

Illustration for an article entitled "Febrile Child," February 15, 1984.

Pencil

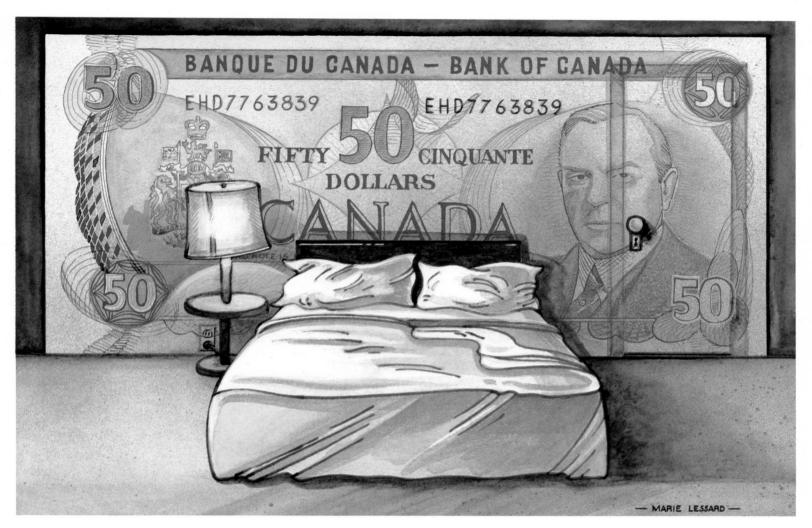

91 ARTIST/DESIGNER
MARIE LESSARD

PUBLICATION
LA PRESSE/PLUS

PUBLISHER
LA PRESSE LIMITÉE

Cover illustration for a story on prostitution,
February 16, 1985.

Mixed media

92   Artist/Designer
PATRICK LYNN CARSON

Graphics Coordinator
KEVIN MURPHY

Publication
NORTHWEST MAGAZINE

Publisher
OREGONIAN PUBLISHING COMPANY

Writer
ALICE ADAMS

Illustration for a fiction piece entitled "You Are What You Own," April 8, 1984.

Acrylic and gouache

93 ARTIST
JEFF JACKSON

DESIGNER/ART DIRECTOR
TERESA FERNANDES

PUBLICATION
EXECUTIVE

PUBLISHER
AIRMEDIA LTD.

WRITER
ANDREW WEINER

Cover illustration for an article entitled "From the Ground Up—Lessons in Building an Organization," February 1985.

Gouache and mixed media

94 ARTIST
ALAN E. COBER

DESIGNER
MARK ULRICH

ART EDITOR
PETER DEUTSCH

PUBLICATION
AT&T MAGAZINE

WRITER
BOB KINKEAD

Illustration for an article entitled
"Eyes & Ears on Others," December 1984.

Mixed media

95 ARTIST
ALAN E. COBER

DESIGNERS
TERRY BROWN/JUDY GARLAN

ART DIRECTORS
TERRY BROWN/JUDY GARLAN

PUBLICATION
THE ATLANTIC

PUBLISHER
THE ATLANTIC MONTHLY CO.

WRITER
PETER HELLMAN

Illustration for an article entitled
"Israel's Chariot of Fire," March 1985.

Pen and ink, watercolor, pencil, and letraset

96 ARTIST
GARY KELLEY

DESIGNERS
FRED WOODWARD/DAVID KAMPA

ART DIRECTOR
FRED WOODWARD

PUBLICATION
TEXAS MONTHLY

PUBLISHER
TEXAS MONTHLY, INC.

WRITER
STEPHEN HARRIGAN

Illustration for an article entitled "Texas Primer: The Yellow Rose of Texas," April 1984.

Pastel

97 ARTIST
GREG SPALENKA

ART DIRECTORS
DEBORAH STAIRS/LAURA LAMAR

PUBLICATION
SAN FRANCISCO FOCUS

PUBLISHER
KQED INC.

WRITER
CARL HEINTZE

Illustration for an article entitled
"The Garbageman's Daughter,"
October 1984.

Oil and acrylic

98 ARTIST
BONNIE TIMMONS

DESIGNER
GAYLE SIMS

ART DIRECTOR
DAVID MILLER

PUBLICATION
CONTEMPORARY MAGAZINE

PUBLISHER
THE DENVER POST

WRITER
MARILYN MANSFIELD

Illustration for an article entitled "Your Gay Child," August 1984.

Ink and marker

99 ARTIST
JOHN HERSEY

ART DIRECTOR
BRUCE CHARONNAT

PUBLICATION
MACWORLD MAGAZINE

PUBLISHER
PC WORLD COMMUNICATIONS, INC.

WRITER
BILL GROUT

Illustration for an article entitled "Just the Facts," February 1985.

Computer

100 ARTIST
BRAD HOLLAND

ART EDITOR
WALTER HERDEG

PUBLICATION
GRAPHIS

PUBLISHER
THE GRAPHIS PRESS CORP.

WRITER
STEVEN HELLER

Cover illustration for an article about the
artist's work, March 1985.

Acrylic on masonite

101 ARTIST
BRAD HOLLAND

DESIGNER
KERIG POPE

ART DIRECTORS
TOM STAEBLER/KERIG POPE

PUBLICATION
PLAYBOY

PUBLISHER
PLAYBOY ENTERPRISES, INC.

WRITER
LAURENCE GONZALES

Illustration for an article entitled "Cocaine,"
September 1984.

Acrylic on masonite

102 ARTIST
MICHAEL C. WITTE

ART DIRECTOR
JUDY GARLAN

PUBLICATION
THE ATLANTIC

PUBLISHER
THE ATLANTIC MONTHLY CO.

WRITER
GREGG EASTERBROOK

Cover illustration for an article entitled
"What's Wrong With Congress," December
1984.

Watercolor, prismacolor pencil, and pen and
ink

103 ARTIST/WRITER
EDWARD SOREL

DESIGNER
JUSTINE STRASBERG

ART DIRECTOR
JAY PURVIS

PUBLICATION
GENTLEMAN'S QUARTERLY

PUBLISHER
CONDÉ NAST PUBLICATIONS

Illustration for an article by the artist entitled
"Keyhole History," October 1984.

Pen and ink and watercolor

104 ARTIST
CATHY BARANCIK

DESIGNER/ART DIRECTOR
RONN CAMPISI

PUBLICATION
THE BOSTON GLOBE MAGAZINE

PUBLISHER
AFFILIATED PUBLICATIONS

WRITER
ALICE KOLLER

Illustration for an article entitled
"Reflections While Gathering Wild
Raspberries," July 15, 1984.

Pastel

105 ARTIST
CATHY BARANCIK

ART DIRECTOR
TOM RUIS

PUBLICATION
DAILY NEWS

WRITER
MICHAEL McLAUGHLIN

Illustration for an article entitled "A Berry
Nice Gift," December 9, 1984.

Pastel

106 ARTIST
SALVADOR BRU

DESIGNER/ART DIRECTOR
GARY BERNLOEHR

PUBLICATION
FLORIDA TREND MAGAZINE

PUBLISHER
FLORIDA TREND MAGAZINE

WRITER
THOMAS J. BILLITTERI

Illustration for an article entitled "Is the Bullet Train More Than Just a Shot in the Dark," February 1985.

Gouache and colored pencil

107 ARTIST
KEN MARYANSKI

ART DIRECTOR
STAN McCRAY

PUBLICATION
BOSTON MAGAZINE

WRITER
KATE BROUGHTON

Illustration for an article entitled "Chef's
Night Out," July 1984.

Watercolor

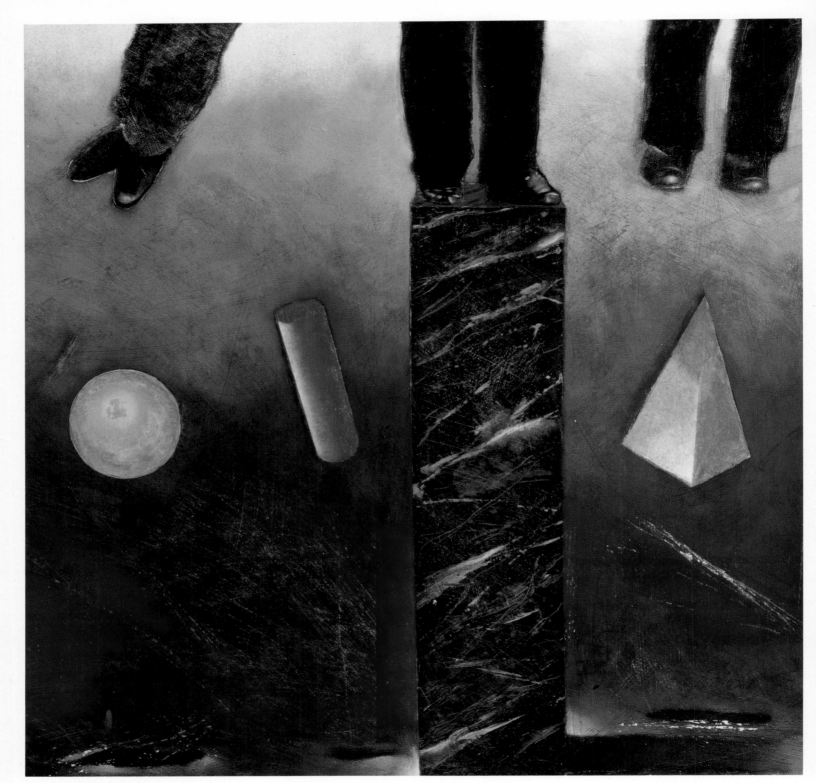

108 ARTIST
MARK PENBERTHY

CREATIVE DIRECTOR
PETER J. BLANK

ART DIRECTOR
MARY ZISK

PUBLICATION
PC MAGAZINE

PUBLISHER
ZIFF-DAVIS PUBLISHING CO.

WRITER
GEORGE C. HAYLES

Illustration for an article on software entitled
"Sticking to Fundamentals," July 10, 1984.

Oil

109 ARTIST
MARK PENBERTHY

CREATIVE DIRECTOR
PETER J. BLANK

ART DIRECTORS
MITCH SHOSTAK/MARY ZISK

PUBLICATION
PC MAGAZINE

PUBLISHER
ZIFF-DAVIS PUBLISHING CO.

WRITER
GEORGE C. HAYLES

Illustration for an article entitled "Dialing for
Financial Data," October 16, 1984.

Oil

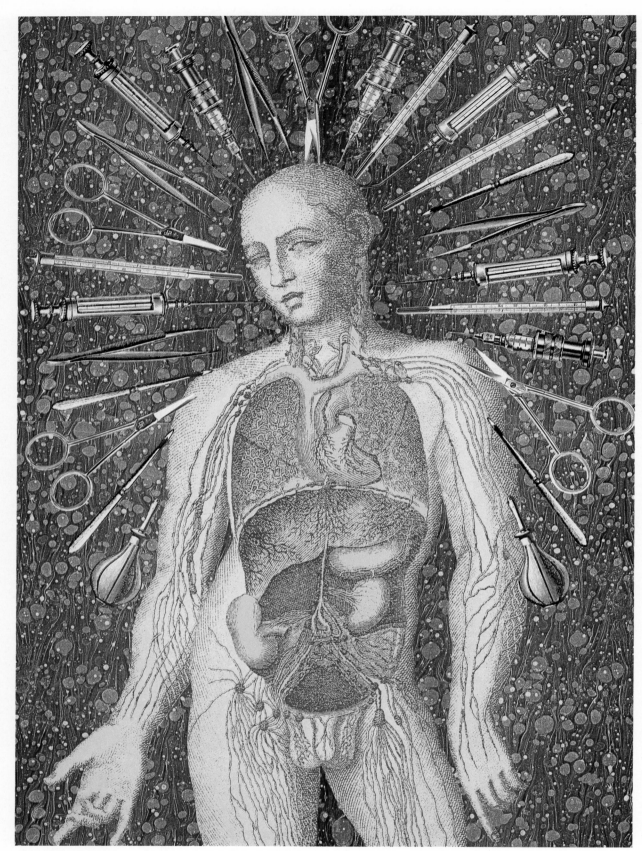

110 ARTIST
MELISSA GRIMES

DESIGNER/ART DIRECTOR
BILL HEWSON

PUBLICATION
THE TEXAS HUMANIST

PUBLISHER
TEXAS COMMISSION FOR THE HUMANITIES

WRITER
JOEL BARNA

Illustration for an article about prolonging life
artificially entitled "The Texas Natural Death
Act," May/June 1984.

Collage

111 ARTIST
JOHN CRAIG

ART DIRECTOR
GREG PAUL

PUBLICATION
SUNSHINE MAGAZINE

PUBLISHER
FT. LAUDERDALE NEWS & SUN SENTINEL

Portrait of a baseball trivia expert, March
1984.

Collage and overlays

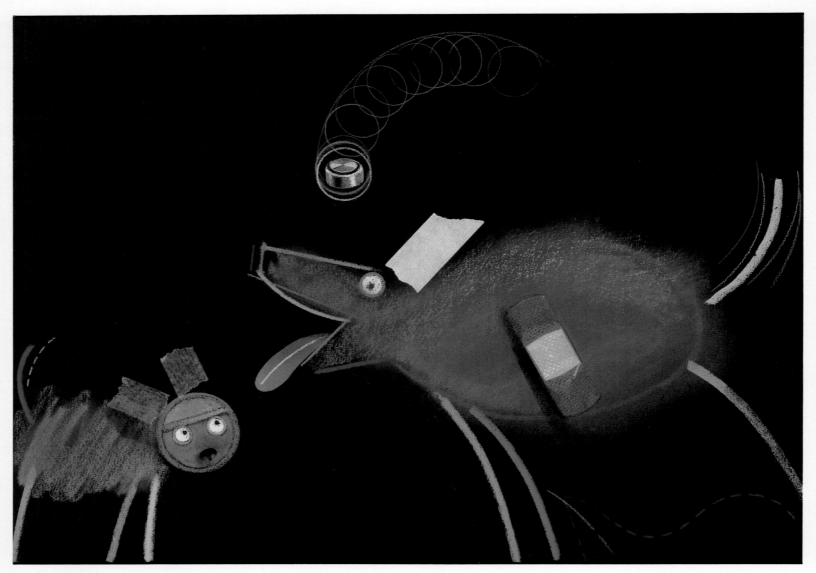

112 ARTIST
ANDRZEJ DUDZINSKI

DESIGNER/ART DIRECTOR
WAYNE FITZPATRICK

PUBLICATION
SCIENCE 85 MAGAZINE

PUBLISHER
AMERICAN ASSOCIATION FOR THE ADVANCEMENT OF SCIENCE

WRITER
SARAH RABKIN

Illustration for an article entitled "Pacemakers: Going to the Dogs," February 1985.

Mixed media

113 ARTIST
MARIE-LOUISE GAY

ART DIRECTOR
HAMO ABDALIAN

PUBLICATION
MONTREAL CALENDAR MAGAZINE

PUBLISHER
MONTREAL CALENDAR MAGAZINE

Cover illustration for a travel feature entitled
"Great Spring Get-Aways," May 1984.

Scratchboard, dye, and collage

114 ARTIST
JULIAN ALLEN

DESIGNER
CHARLES BRUCALIERE

ART DIRECTOR
APRIL SILVER

PUBLICATION
ESQUIRE

PUBLISHER
ESQUIRE ASSOCIATES INC.

WRITER
JERROLD L. SCHECTER

Illustration for an article entitled "Democracy
Comes for the Argentines," July 1984.

Charcoal

115 ARTIST
VIVIENNE FLESHER

DESIGNER/ART DIRECTOR
RONN CAMPISI

PUBLICATION
THE BOSTON GLOBE MAGAZINE

PUBLISHER
AFFILIATED PUBLICATIONS

WRITER
RICHARD DYER

Portrait for an article entitled "Mable Mercer:
A Remembrance," June 3, 1984.

Charcoal

116 ARTIST/DESIGNER
GENE GARBOWSKI

ART DIRECTOR
JANE PALECEK

PUBLICATION
THE WASHINGTON TIMES

PUBLISHER
THE WASHINGTON TIMES

WRITER
W.J. ELVIN III

Illustration for an article entitled "Raiding Indian Graveyards," January 10, 1985.

Watercolor and airbrush

117 ARTIST
MARCIA STIEGER

ART DIRECTOR
MICK WIGGINS

PUBLICATION
PC WORLD

PUBLISHER
PC WORLD COMMUNICATIONS, INC.

Illustration for an article on kitchen
organization through home computers,
February 1985.

Collage

118 ARTIST
DOUG SMITH

DESIGNER/ART DIRECTOR
RONN CAMPISI

PUBLICATION
THE BOSTON GLOBE MAGAZINE

PUBLISHER
AFFILIATED PUBLICATIONS

WRITER
DON SNYDER

Illustration for a story entitled "The Spies
Who Came in From the Coast," October 14,
1984.

Scratchboard

119 ARTIST
CATHIE BLECK

ART DIRECTOR
JAMES NOEL SMITH

PUBLICATION
WESTWARD

PUBLISHER
DALLAS TIMES HERALD

WRITER
JAMES WAKEFIELD BURKE

Cover illustration for a story entitled "David
Crockett—The Man Behind the Myth,"
December 2, 1984.

Ink and scratchboard

120 ARTIST
ROBERT RISKO

DESIGNER
THEO KOUVATSOS

ART DIRECTOR
TOM STAEBLER

PUBLICATION
PLAYBOY

PUBLISHER
PLAYBOY ENTERPRISES, INC.

WRITERS
REGGIE JACKSON/MIKE LUPICA

Portrait for an article entitled "My Life in
Pinstripes," June 1984.

Gouache

121 ARTIST
ROBERT RISKO

DESIGNER
DAVID RIVAS

ART DIRECTOR
RAY WEBSTER

PUBLICATION
IN STYLE

PUBLISHER
IN TOUCH INTERNATIONAL

WRITER
CLAIR PETERSON

Caricature for an article entitled "Truman
Capote Remembered," February 1985.

Gouache

122 ARTIST
DAVID SHANNON

ART DIRECTOR
JOHN McLEOD

PUBLICATION
INX NEWS GRAPHICS

PUBLISHER
UNITED FEATURE SYNDICATE

Illustration entitled "Missile-ing the Point" depicting the lack of communication in arms talks, October 4, 1985.

Acrylic

123 ARTIST
DAVID SHANNON

ART DIRECTOR
ROBERT NEUBECKER

PUBLICATION
INX NEWS GRAPHICS

PUBLISHER
UNITED FEATURE SYNDICATE

Illustration entitled "Shelter from the Storm"
depicting the resumption of arms
negotiations, January 30, 1985.

Acrylic

124 ARTIST
BILL VUKSANOVICH

ART DIRECTOR
RICHARD WHITTINGTON

PUBLICATION
THE TEXAS HUMANIST

PUBLISHER
TEXAS COMMISSION FOR THE HUMANITIES

WRITER
JAMES HILLMAN

Illustration for an article entitled "Extending
the Family: From Entrapment to Embrace,"
March/April 1985.

Oil

SPALENKA

125 ARTIST
GREG SPALENKA

ART DIRECTOR
GERARD SEALY

PUBLICATION
THE PLAIN DEALER MAGAZINE

PUBLISHER
THE PLAIN DEALER PUBLISHING CO.

WRITER
DAISY LEE DONALDSON

Cover illustration for "A Diary," the author's
recollections of farm life in old Ohio,
November 18, 1984.

Oil

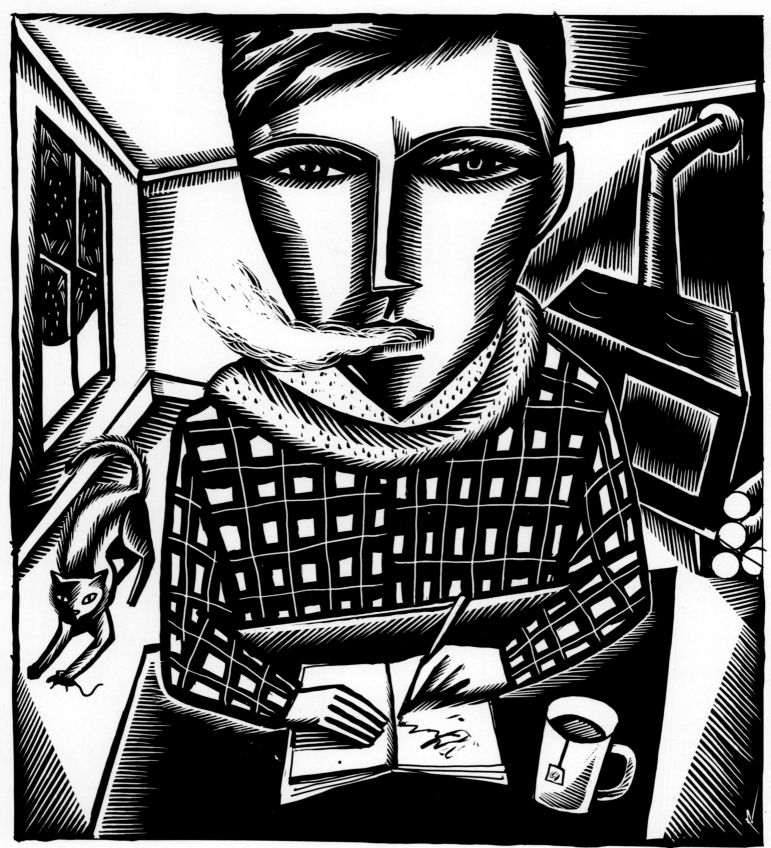

126 ARTIST
ANTHONY RUSSO

DESIGNER/ART DIRECTOR
RONN CAMPISI

PUBLICATION
THE BOSTON GLOBE MAGAZINE

PUBLISHER
AFFILIATED PUBLICATIONS

WRITER
JOHN MORRISSEY

Illustration for an article entitled "Haywards
Country Journal," December 30, 1984.

Scratchboard

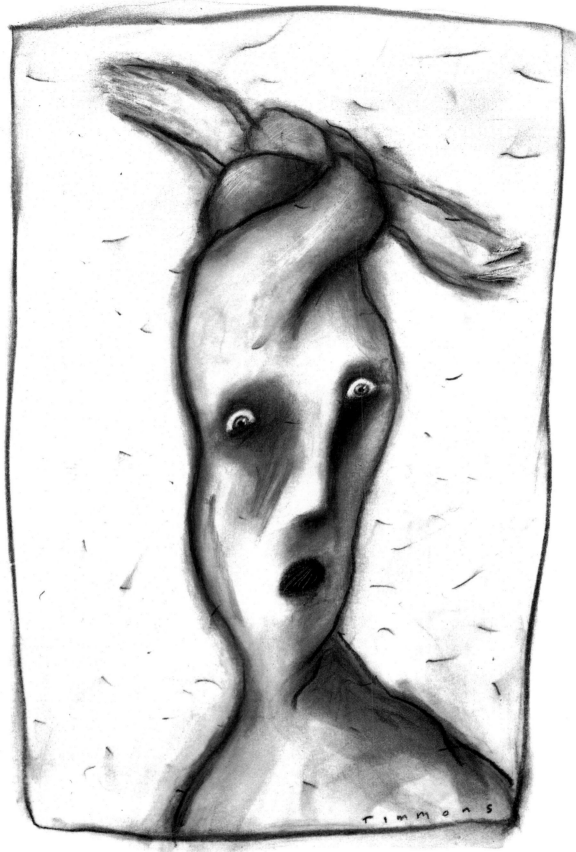

127 ARTIST
BONNIE TIMMONS

DESIGNER
GAYLE SIMS

ART DIRECTOR
RANDY MILLER

PUBLICATION
CONTEMPORARY MAGAZINE

PUBLISHER
THE DENVER POST

Illustration for an article entitled "Migraines: Biology or Destiny," 1984.

Pastel

128 ARTIST
PAUL MEISEL

DESIGNER
DAVID STEINLICHT

ART DIRECTOR
BARBARA KOSTER

PUBLICATION
TWA AMBASSADOR

PUBLISHER
PAULSEN PUBLISHING COMPANY

WRITER
NAO HAUSER

Illustration for an article entitled "The Global Kitchen," February 1985.

Watercolor

129 ARTIST
TRACI HAYMANS

DESIGNER/ART DIRECTOR
PEGGY ROBERTSON

PUBLICATION
ATLANTA WEEKLY MAGAZINE

PUBLISHER
ATLANTA JOURNAL AND CONSTITUTION

WRITERS
EDGAR AND PATRICIA CHEATHAM

Illustration for an article entitled "Traveling
in Paris," March 24, 1985.

Pastel and colored pencil

130 ARTIST
BUDDY HICKERSON

ART DIRECTOR
JAMES NOEL SMITH

PUBLICATION
WESTWARD

PUBLISHER
DALLAS TIMES HERALD

Illustration for a listing of amusement parks in
Dallas for the Republic Convention issue,
August 19, 1984.

Mixed media

131 ARTIST
KRISTOPHER COPELAND

DESIGNER
JENNY KENNEDY

ART DIRECTORS
KRISTOPHER COPELAND/JENNY KENNEDY

PUBLICATION
SUNDAY MAGAZINE

PUBLISHER
S&T PUBLISHING

Illustration for an article entitled "My
Apartment," January 1985.

Oil

132 ARTIST
ALEX MURAWSKI

ART DIRECTOR
DAVID HERBICK

PUBLICATION
GAMES MAGAZINE

PUBLISHER
PLAYBOY ENTERPRISES, INC.

A hidden image puzzle, July 1984.

Watercolor with black overlay

133 ARTIST
DOUG SMITH

DESIGNER/ART DIRECTOR
JOHN HAROLD

PUBLICATION
ULTRASPORT

PUBLISHER
RABEN/ULTRASPORT PARTNERS

WRITER
WILLIAM PUGSLEY

Illustration for a fiction piece entitled
"Choices of Men," March/April 1985.

Scratchboard and watercolor

134 ARTIST
BOB ZUBA

ART DIRECTOR
MURRY KEITH

PUBLICATION
MEMPHIS MAGAZINE

PUBLISHER
TOWERY PRESS, INC.

WRITER
MARY LOVELESS

Illustration for an article on diet pills entitled
"Fat Chance," November 1984.

Liquitex acrylic color

135 ARTIST/DESIGNER
DUGALD STERMER

ART DIRECTOR
VERONIQUE VIENNE

PUBLICATION
WEST

PUBLISHER
SAN JOSE MERCURY NEWS

Cover illustration for an article entitled "Ed Meese: Over His Head," March 25, 1984.

Pencil and watercolor on arches paper

136 ARTIST
SEAN EARLEY

ART DIRECTOR
STAN McCRAY

PUBLICATION
BOSTON MAGAZINE

WRITER
TED WILLIAMS

Illustration for an article on the mercy killing
of deer in New Hampshire entitled "Should
They Shoot Bambi," November 1984.

Acrylic paint

137 ARTIST
RICHARD McNEEL

DESIGNER/ART DIRECTOR
RONN CAMPISI

PUBLICATION
THE BOSTON GLOBE MAGAZINE

PUBLISHER
AFFILIATED PUBLICATIONS

WRITER
PETER ANDERSON

Cover illustration for an article on the modern
dairy farmer entitled "In the Land of Milk and
Honey," February 3, 1985.

Sculptured illustration

138 ARTIST
DAVID H. COWLES

DESIGNER
RANDY MEDEMA

PUBLICATION
DEMOCRAT AND CHRONICLE

PUBLISHER
GANNETT ROCHESTER NEWSPAPERS

Illustration for "Black History Month,"
January 30, 1985.

Watercolor and colored pencil

139 ARTIST
SARA SCHWARTZ

DESIGNER/ART DIRECTOR
AMY SUSSMAN HEIT

PUBLICATION
ART DIRECTION MAGAZINE

PUBLISHER
ADVERTISING TRADE PUBLICATIONS INC.

WRITER
MARY YEUNG

Illustration for a story on the artist's work,
September 1984.

Colored pencil

140 ARTIST/DESIGNER/ART DIRECTOR
JIM BUCKELS

PUBLICATION
WALLACES FARMER

PUBLISHER
WALLACE-HOMESTEAD CO.

Cover illustration, January 12, 1985.

Airbrush and acrylic

141 ARTIST
DAVE CALVER

ART DIRECTORS
ROBERT BEST/PATRICIA VON BRACHEL

PUBLICATION
NEW YORK MAGAZINE

PUBLISHER
MURDOCH MAGAZINES

WRITERS
NANCY McKEON/CORKY POLLAN

Cover illustration for a feature entitled
"Christmas Gifts," December 3, 1984.

Colored pencil

142 ARTIST
PETER DE SEVE

ART DIRECTORS
ROBERT BEST/PATRICIA VON BRACHEL

PUBLICATION
NEW YORK MAGAZINE

PUBLISHER
MURDOCH MAGAZINES

WRITER
DINITIA SMITH

Illustration for an article on con artists
entitled "The Man From Angola," January 23,
1984.

Watercolor

143 ARTIST
PETER DE SÈVE

ART DIRECTOR
ELIZABETH WILLIAMS

PUBLICATION
ROLLING STONE YEARBOOK 1984

PUBLISHER
STRAIGHT ARROW PUBLISHERS INC.

WRITER
TOM WOLFE

Illustration for a story entitled "Bonfire of the Vanities."

Watercolor

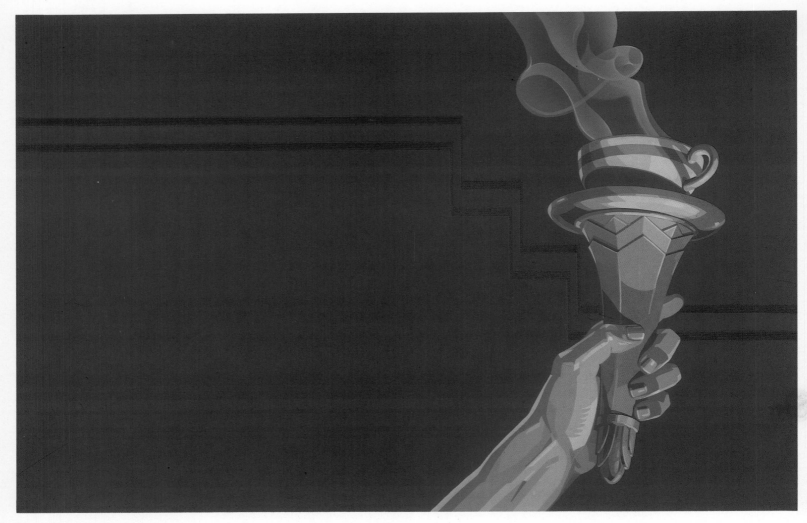

144 ARTIST
NANCY STAHL

ART DIRECTOR
CRAIG BERNHARDT

PUBLICATION
MAXWELL HOUSE MESSENGER

PUBLISHER
MAXWELL HOUSE/GENERAL FOODS CORP.

WRITER
NAN HALEY REDMOND

Cover illustration for an article entitled
"Maxwell House Pride," Fall 1984/Winter
1985.

Gouache

145 ARTIST
LAURA SMITH

ART DIRECTOR
LEE ANN JAFFEE

PUBLICATION
MEETINGS & CONVENTIONS MAGAZINE

PUBLISHER
ZIFF-DAVIS PUBLISHING CO.

WRITER
STELLA JOHNSON

Illustration for an article entitled "Hotels in Downtown New York," May 1984.

Gouache

SOVIET·FIT·NESS

146 ARTIST
PAUL ROGERS

ART DIRECTOR
JEFF BYERS

PUBLICATION
SPORTS FITNESS MAGAZINE

PUBLISHER
JOE WEIDER PUBLISHING

WRITER
MICHAEL YESSIS

Illustration for an article entitled
"Soviet Sports and the Great Cradle Robbery,"
March 1985.

Mixed media

147 ARTIST
GAIL GELTNER

DESIGNER
JOLENE CUYLER

ART DIRECTOR
LOUIS FISHAUF

PUBLICATION
SATURDAY NIGHT

PUBLISHER
SATURDAY NIGHT PUBLISHING

WRITER
JAMES GILLIES

Illustration for an article entitled "The Parliamentary Imperative," June 1984.

Ink

148 ARTIST
TIP TOLAND

PUBLICATION
PACIFIC NORTHWEST

PUBLISHER
PACIFIC SEARCH PUBLICATIONS

WRITER
FRED MOODY

Illustration for an article entitled "The Ties
That Bind," January/February 1985.

Bas-relief ceramic

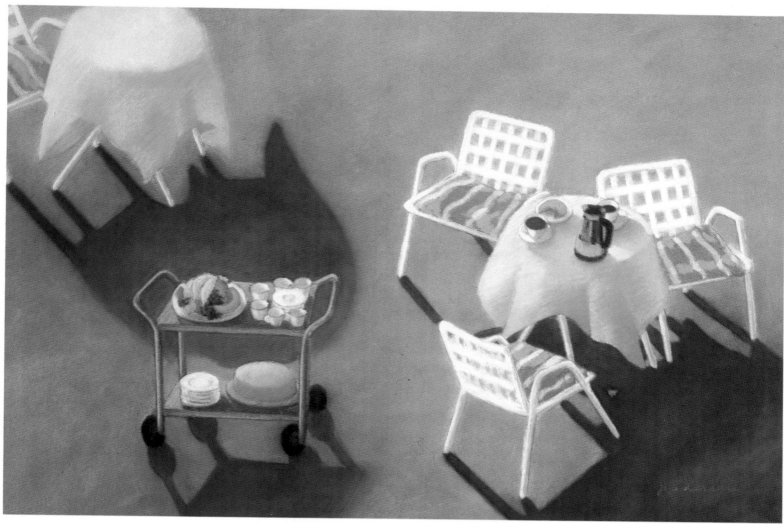

149 ARTIST
JUDY PEDERSEN

ART DIRECTORS
JANICE FUDYMA/CRAIG BERNHARDT

PUBLICATION
MAXWELL HOUSE MESSENGER

PUBLISHER
MAXWELL HOUSE/GENERAL FOODS CORP.

Cover illustration depicting the world-wide
appeal of coffee, 1984.

Pastel

MATTELSON

150 ARTIST
MARVIN MATTELSON

DESIGNER/ART DIRECTOR
BOB EICHINGER

PUBLICATION
REACH MAGAZINE

PUBLISHER
ST. REGIS CORPORATON

WRITER
ELLIS COWLING

Illustration for an article entitled "Acid
Rain," Summer 1984.

Acrylic

151 ARTIST
MARVIN MATTELSON

DESIGNERS
WALTER BERNARD/MILTON GLASER

ART DIRECTOR
DON McCARTEN

PUBLICATION
U.S. NEWS & WORLD REPORT

PUBLISHER
U.S. NEWS & WORLD REPORT

Cover illustration for an article entitled "The
Marxist World—Lure of Capitalism,"
February 4, 1985.

Acrylic

152　ARTIST
ROBERT M. CUNNINGHAM

ART DIRECTOR
HARVEY GRUT

PUBLICATION
SPORTS ILLUSTRATED

PUBLISHER
TIME INC.

Illustration for an article entitled "Summer Camp," July 23, 1984.
Acrylic on paper

153 ARTIST
TERRY WIDENER

ART DIRECTORS
DIANE MARINCE/MIKE FULD

PUBLICATION
AMERICAN WAY MAGAZINE

PUBLISHER
AMERICAN AIRLINES

WRITER
MICHAEL FORMAN

Illustration for an article entitled "Pressure
Points," October 1984.

Oil

154 ARTIST
JEFF SMITH

ART DIRECTOR
KEN KENDRICK

PUBLICATION
NEW YORK TIMES MAGAZINE

PUBLISHER
THE NEW YORK TIMES

WRITER
GEORGE VECSEY

Illustration for an article entitled
"Growing Up Together," April 29, 1984.

Watercolor

155 ARTIST
PAT CUMMINGS

DESIGNER
MARLOWE GOODSON

ART DIRECTOR
FO WILSON

PUBLICATION
ESSENCE MAGAZINE

PUBLISHER
ESSENCE COMMUNICATIONS, INC.

WRITER
ORALEE WACHTER

Illustration for a story entitled "Promise Not to Tell," June 1984.

Mixed media

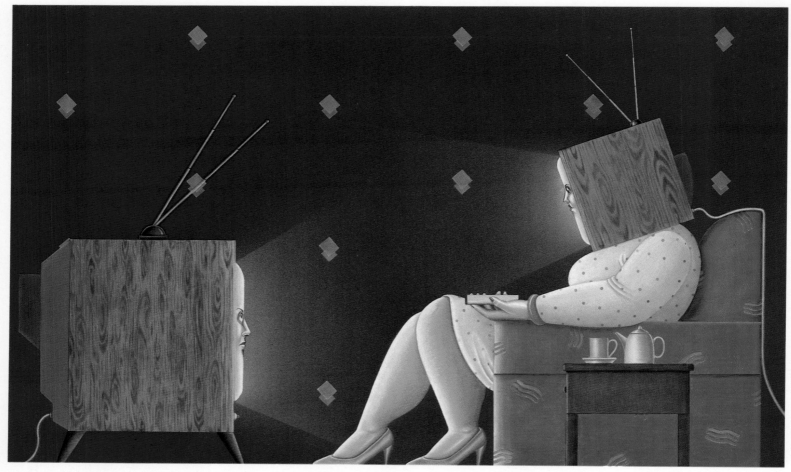

156 ARTIST/DESIGNER
SANDRA HENDLER

ART DIRECTOR
DAVID HERBICK

PUBLICATION
GAMES MAGAZINE

PUBLISHER
PLAYBOY ENTERPRISES, INC.

WRITERS
STEPHANIE SPADACCINI/CURTIS SLEPIAN

Illustration for an article entitled "Watching
Television Watching You," February 1984.

Gouache and colored pencil

157 ARTIST
PATTY DRYDEN

ART DIRECTORS
ROBERT BEST/PATRICIA VON BRACHEL

PUBLICATION
NEW YORK MAGAZINE

PUBLISHER
MURDOCH MAGAZINES

WRITER
PATRICIA MORRISROE

Illustration for an article entitled "Forever
Single," August 20, 1984.

Pastel

158 ARTIST
SEAN EARLEY

ART DIRECTOR
JAMES NOEL SMITH

PUBLICATION
WESTWARD

PUBLISHER
DALLAS TIMES HERALD

WRITER
MARY BARRINEAU

Cover illustration for a story about Alcoholics
Anonymous, June 3, 1984.

Gouache

159 ARTIST
KEVIN LYLES

DESIGNER
JOHN MILLER

ART DIRECTOR
APRIL SILVER

PUBLICATION
ESQUIRE

PUBLISHER
ESQUIRE ASSOCIATES INC.

WRITER
ROBERT STONE

Illustration for an article entitled "Not for
Love," August 1984.

Watercolor

160 ARTIST
JEAN TUTTLE

DESIGNER
ANN DuVIVIER

ART DIRECTOR
LESTER GOODMAN

PUBLICATION
PSYCHOLOGY TODAY

PUBLISHER
AMERICAN PSYCHOLOGICAL ASSOCIATION

WRITER
SCOTT HAAS

Illustration for a book review entitled "The
Nuclear State: Hope in the Face of Danger,"
April 1984.

Scratchboard with mechanical color

161 ARTIST
JEAN TUTTLE

DESIGNER
JOLENE CUYLER

ART DIRECTOR
LOUIS FISHAUF

PUBLICATION
SATURDAY NIGHT

PUBLISHER
SATURDAY NIGHT PUBLISHING

WRITER
NEIL BISSOONDATH

Illustration for a fiction piece entitled
"Dancing," February 1985.

Scratchboard and mechanical color

162 ARTIST
DAVID SHANNON

ART DIRECTOR
STEVEN HELLER

PUBLICATION
NEW YORK TIMES BOOK REVIEW

PUBLISHER
THE NEW YORK TIMES

WRITER
RICHARD LOCKE

Illustration for a book review entitled "Down and Out in Paris," July 22, 1984.

Acrylic

163 ARTIST
CATHIE BLECK

DESIGNER/ART DIRECTOR
MARTY BRAUN

PUBLICATION
THE BOSTON GLOBE MAGAZINE

PUBLISHER
AFFILIATED PUBLICATIONS

WRITER
MARGARET MANNING

Illustration for a book review.entitled "Two
Narratives from V.S. Naipaul," September
16, 1984.

Scratchboard

164 ARTIST
WARD SCHUMAKER

ART DIRECTOR
VERONIQUE VIENNE

PUBLICATION
GREAT ESCAPES/CALIFORNIA LIVING MAGAZINE

PUBLISHER
SAN FRANCISCO EXAMINER

WRITER
JESSICA MITFORD

Portrait of the writer for an article entitled
"The Saga of Swinbrook," March 24, 1985.

Colored pencil

167 ARTIST
PHILIPPE WEISBECKER

DESIGNER
ANTHONY RUSSELL

PUBLICATION
FINANCIAL ENTERPRISE

PUBLISHER
GENERAL ELECTRIC CREDIT CORP.

WRITER
KARL A. VESPER

Illustration for an article entitled
"Entrepreneurship/Nine Issues and Two
Questions," Winter 1984.
Ink and watercolor

168 ARTIST
JOSÉ CRUZ

ART DIRECTOR
HANS-GEORG POSPISCHIL

PUBLICATION
FRANKFURTER ALLGEMEINE MAGAZIN

PUBLISHER
FRANKFURTER ALLGEMEINE ZEITUNG GmbH.

WRITER
UDO PINI

One in a series of illustrations for an article
entitled "Santa Claus is Coming Tomorrow,"
December 21, 1984.

Gouache and mixed media

169 ARTIST
CHRISTOPH BLUMRICH

ART DIRECTOR
HANS-GEORG POSPISCHIL

PUBLICATION
FRANKFURTER ALLGEMEINE MAGAZIN

PUBLISHER
FRANKFURTER ALLGEMEINE ZEITUNG GmbH.

WRITER
UDO PINI

One in a series of illustrations for an article
entitled "Santa Claus is Coming Tomorrow,"
December 21, 1984.

Tempera

170 ARTIST
CARTER GOODRICH

CREATIVE DIRECTOR
PETER J. BLANK

ART DIRECTOR
MARY ZISK

PUBLICATION
PC MAGAZINE

PUBLISHER
ZIFF-DAVIS PUBLISHING CO.

WRITERS
G. WILLIAM DAUPHINAIS/GLEN SELLER

Illustration for an article entitled "Accounting
for Individual Tastes," February 19, 1985.

Prismacolor

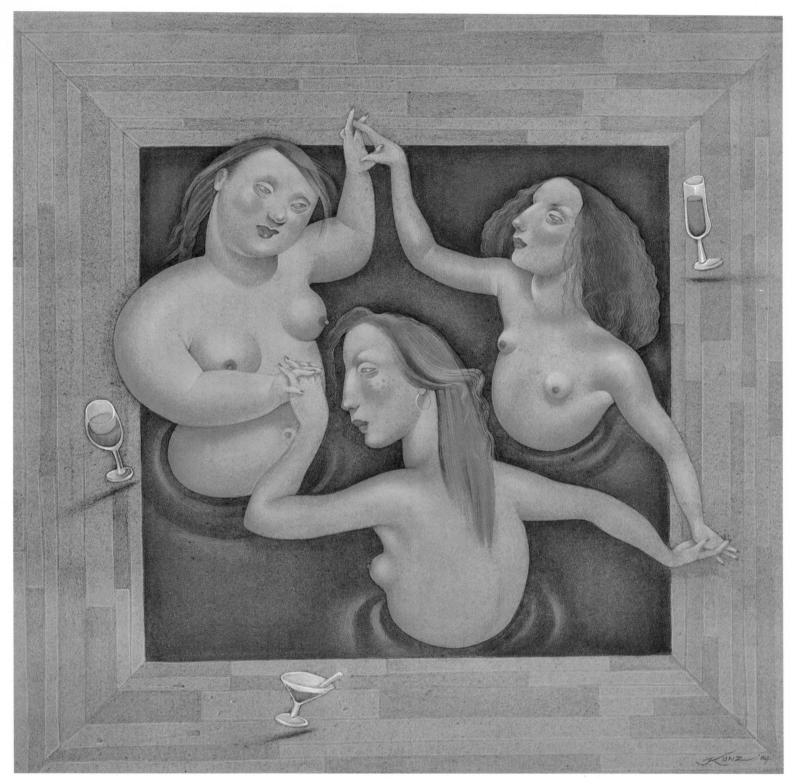

171 ARTIST
ANITA KUNZ

DESIGNER
KERIG POPE

ART DIRECTOR
TOM STAEBLER

PUBLICATION
PLAYBOY

PUBLISHER
PLAYBOY ENTERPRISES, INC.

WRITER
JOHN UPDIKE

Illustration for the story entitled "The Witches of Eastwick," May 1984.

Watercolor and gouache

172 ARTIST
WENDY BURDEN

ART DIRECTOR
PAULA GREIF

PUBLICATION
MADEMOISELLE

PUBLISHER
CONDÉ NAST PUBLICATIONS

Illustration for an article entitled "Salad
Stars," May 1984.

Oil pastel

173 ARTIST
NANCY STAHL

ART DIRECTOR
TOM BODKIN

PUBLICATION
THE SOPHISTICATED TRAVELER

PUBLISHER
THE NEW YORK TIMES

Cover illustration, March 18, 1984.

Dye and colored pencil

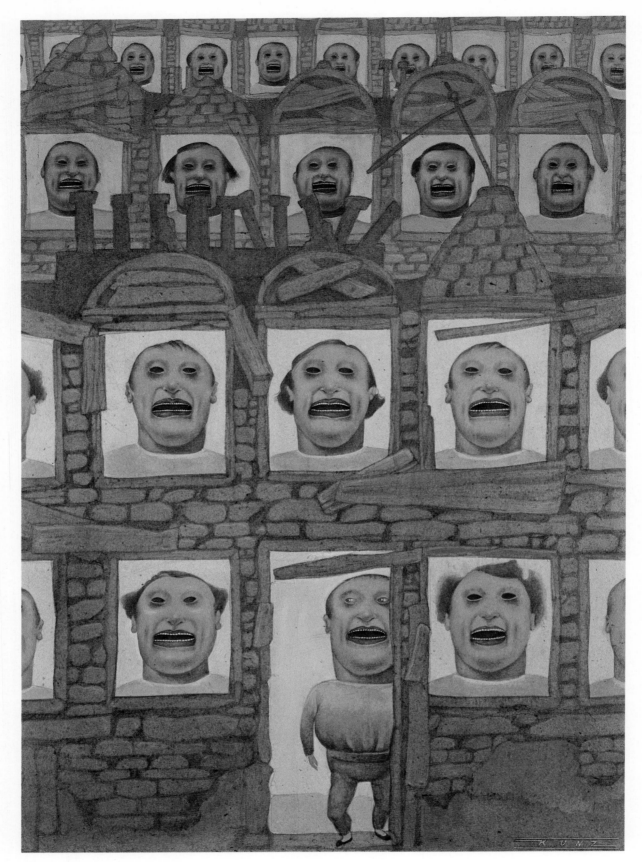

174 ARTIST
ANITA KUNZ

DESIGNER/ART DIRECTOR
ART NIEMI

PUBLICATION
QUEST

PUBLISHER
COMAC COMMUNICATIONS LTD.

Illustration for an article entitled "1984,"
Spring 1984.

Watercolor and gouache

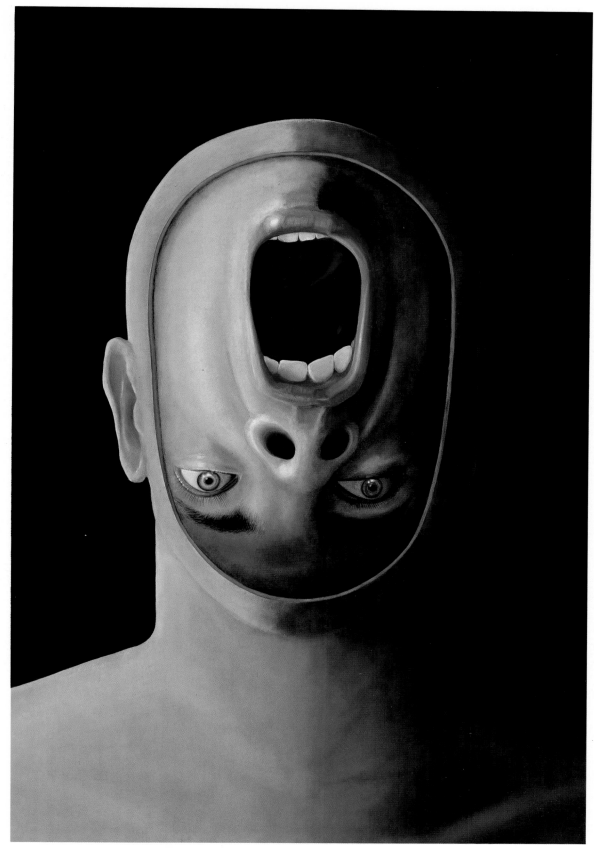

175 ARTIST
JEAN-FRANCOIS PODEVIN

ART DIRECTOR
PRISCILLA HANSEN

PUBLICATION
THE BOOK REVIEW

PUBLISHER
LOS ANGELES TIMES

WRITER
WARREN BENNIS

Illustration for an article entitled "The Very
Concept of Truth As Now Condensed," 1984.
Oil

176 ARTIST
GARY KELLEY

DESIGNERS
GARY BERNLOEHR/GARY KELLEY

ART DIRECTOR
GARY BERNLOEHR

PUBLICATION
FLORIDA TREND MAGAZINE

PUBLISHER
FLORIDA TREND MAGAZINE

WRITER
PENNY LERNOUX

Illustration for an article entitled "When it
Comes to Buying a Bank, Anyone Goes,"
April 1984.

Pastel

れっじい すみす

177 ARTIST
KINUKO Y. CRAFT

DESIGNER
BRUCE HANSEN

ART DIRECTOR
TOM STAEBLER

PUBLICATION
PLAYBOY

PUBLISHER
PLAYBOY ENTERPRISES, INC.

WRITER
DAVID HALBERSTAM

Illustration for an article entitled "The
Education of Reggie Smith," October 1984.

Acrylic

178 ARTIST
BUDDY HICKERSON

ART DIRECTOR
JAMES NOEL SMITH

PUBLICATION
WESTWARD

PUBLISHER
DALLAS TIMES HERALD

WRITER
PHILLIP LOPATE

Illustration for an article entitled "Nuptials,"
May 20, 1984.

Mixed media

179 ARTIST
LANE SMITH

ART DIRECTOR
ROBERT PRIEST

PUBLICATION
NEWSWEEK

PUBLISHER
NEWSWEEK, INC.

GENERAL EDITOR
DENNIS WILLIAMS

Illustration for an article entitled "Why Teachers Fail," September 24, 1984.

Alkyd and collage

180 ARTIST
MARY LYNN BLASUTTA

DESIGNER
MARK ULRICH

ART DIRECTOR
ANTHONY RUSSELL

PUBLICATION
SQUIBBLINE

PUBLISHER
SQUIBB CORPORATION

WRITER
GAIL SOKOLOWSKI

Illustrations for a feature entitled
"For Your Information," Winter 1984.

Watercolor

181 ARTIST
GEORGE MASI

DESIGNER
LEN WILLIS

ART DIRECTOR
TOM STAEBLER

PUBLICATION
PLAYBOY

PUBLISHER
PLAYBOY ENTERPRISES, INC.

Series of drawings for a monthly feature
entitled "Forum Newsfront," 1984.

Mixed media

182   ARTIST
MELANIE MARDER PARKS

DESIGNER
HOWARD KLEIN

ART DIRECTOR
KEN KENDRICK

PUBLICATION
NEW YORK TIMES MAGAZINE

PUBLISHER
THE NEW YORK TIMES

WRITER
THOMAS SIMMONS

Illustration for an article entitled "A Mother's Son," November 4, 1984.

Gouache

183 ARTIST
RANDALL ENOS

DESIGNER
MIKE BRENT

ART DIRECTOR
KATHY BURKE

PUBLICATION
GOLF SHOP OPERATIONS

PUBLISHER
GOLF DIGEST/TENNIS INC.

WRITER
NICK ROMANO

Cover illustration for an article entitled
"Farewell Miami," January 1984.

Lino-cut collage

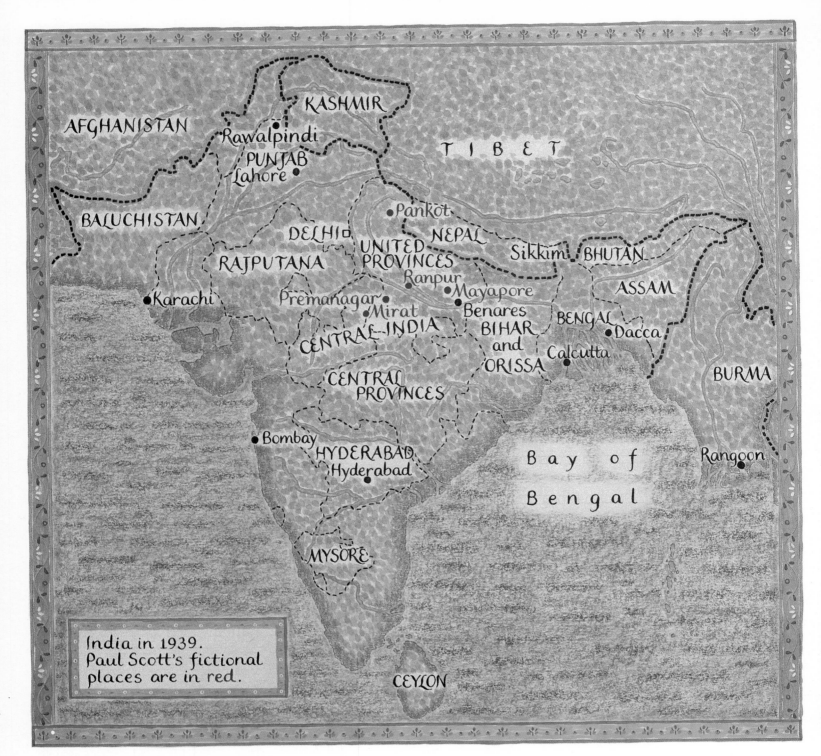

India in 1939.
Paul Scott's fictional
places are in red.

184 ARTIST
MELANIE MARDER PARKS

ART DIRECTOR
BERNARD SCHARF

DESIGN DIRECTOR
GAIL TAUBER

PUBLICATION
THE DIAL

PUBLISHER
EAST WEST NETWORK

WRITER
BARBARA GRIZZUTI HARRISON

Map illustration for an article entitled
"The Enigma of India," December 1984.

Watercolor, colored pencil, and gouache

185 ARTIST
KINUKO Y. CRAFT

DESIGNER
BOB PRATT

ART DIRECTOR
JOHN F. DORR

PUBLICATION
NATIONAL GEOGRAPHIC MAGAZINE

PUBLISHER
NATIONAL GEOGRAPHIC SOCIETY

WRITERS
DOUGLAS LEE/JANE VESSELS

Illustrations for a map showing the history of
Japan, June 1984.

Gouache

186 ARTIST
JAMIE BENNETT

DESIGNER/ART DIRECTOR
TERESA FERNANDES

PUBLICATION
EXECUTIVE

PUBLISHER
AIRMEDIA LTD.

WRITER
MARTIN MEHR

Illustration for an article entitled
"Direct Marketing Hits Home," December
1984.

Watercolor and mixed media

187 ARTIST
BLAIR DRAWSON

DESIGNER
JOLENE CUYLER

ART DIRECTOR
LOUIS FISHAUF

PUBLICATION
SATURDAY NIGHT

PUBLISHER
SATURDAY NIGHT PUBLISHING

WRITER
VAL SEARS

Illustration for a memoir entitled
"The Paper Chase," March 1985.

Watercolor

188 ARTIST
RALPH GIGUERE

DESIGNER/ART DIRECTOR
JUDY GARLAN

PUBLICATION
THE ATLANTIC

PUBLISHER
THE ATLANTIC MONTHLY CO.

WRITER
JANE SMILEY

Illustration for a short story entitled "Lily,"
July 1984.

Pencil

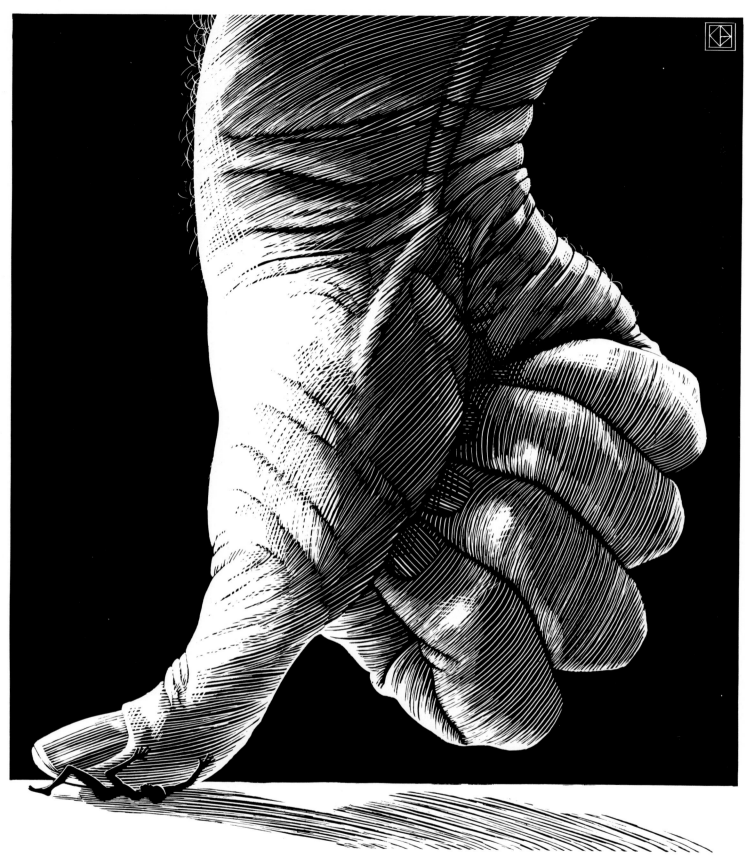

189 ARTIST/ART DIRECTOR
KENT H. BARTON

ART DIRECTORS
RICHARD BARD

PUBLICATION
THE MIAMI HERALD VIEWPOINT

PUBLISHER
THE MIAMI HERALD

WRITER
DESMOND M. TUTU

Illustration for an article entitled "The High Cost of Apartheid," December 16, 1984.

Scraperboard

190 ARTIST
STEVEN GUARNACCIA

DESIGNER/ART DIRECTOR
GERARD SEALY

PUBLICATION
THE PLAIN DEALER MAGAZINE

PUBLISHER
THE PLAIN DEALER PUBLISHING CO.

WRITER
CHRISTOPHER JENSEN

Cover illustration for an article entitled
"Looking for Mr. Goodcar," September 30,
1984.

Pen and ink and watercolor

191 ARTIST
CHERYL COOPER

DESIGNER
BOB PRATT

ART DIRECTOR
JOHN F. DORR

PUBLICATION
NATIONAL GEOGRAPHIC MAGAZINE

PUBLISHER
NATIONAL GEOGRAPHIC SOCIETY

WRITER
GAITHER C. KYHOS

Illustrations for a traveler's map of Spain and
Portugal, October 1984.

Watercolor

S E A N   E A R L E Y

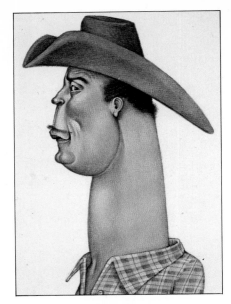

A N I T A   K U N Z

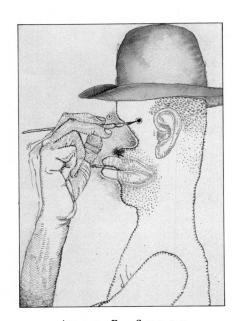

A L A N   E .   C O B E R

A L E X A   G R A C E

192 DESIGNER
DAVID KAMPA

ART DIRECTOR
FRED WOODWARD

PUBLICATION
TEXAS MONTHLY

PUBLISHER
TEXAS MONTHLY, INC.

Twenty different artists "Draw the Cowboy,"
October 1984.

Various media

191 ARTIST
CHERYL COOPER

DESIGNER
BOB PRATT

ART DIRECTOR
JOHN F. DORR

PUBLICATION
NATIONAL GEOGRAPHIC MAGAZINE

PUBLISHER
NATIONAL GEOGRAPHIC SOCIETY

WRITER
GAITHER C. KYHOS

Illustrations for a traveler's map of Spain and
Portugal, October 1984.

Watercolor

S E A N   E A R L E Y

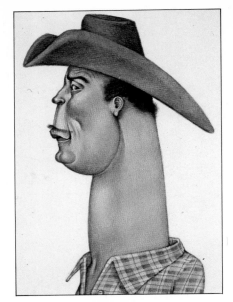

A N I T A   K U N Z

A L A N   E .   C O B E R

A L E X A   G R A C E

192   DESIGNER
DAVID KAMPA

ART DIRECTOR
FRED WOODWARD

PUBLICATION
TEXAS MONTHLY

PUBLISHER
TEXAS MONTHLY, INC.

Twenty different artists "Draw the Cowboy,"
October 1984.

Various media

GARY PANTER

GARY KELLEY

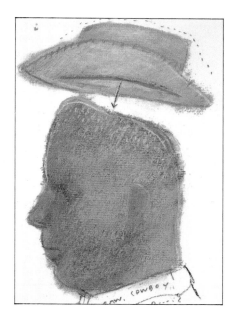

REGAN DUNNICK

THOMAS WOODRUFF

HENRIK DRESCHER

BRAD HOLLAND

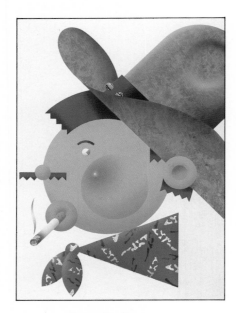

JOSÉ CRUZ

VIVIENNE FLESHER

ANDRZEJ DUDZINSKI

MATT MAHURIN

SUE LLEWELLYN

ELWOOD H. SMITH

195

DAVE CALVER

ALEX MURAWSKI

DAGMAR FRINTA

MARSHALL ARISMAN

196

BOOKS

This section includes cover and inside illustrations for all types
of fiction and non-fiction books.

198 ARTIST
JOHN COLLIER

ART DIRECTOR
MICHAEL MENDELSOHN

AUTHOR
EUDORA WELTY

PUBLISHER
THE FRANKLIN LIBRARY

Illustration for *The Optimist's Daughter*,
published August 1985.

Monoprint

199 ARTIST
BRAD HOLLAND

DESIGNER/ART DIRECTOR
LOUISE FILI

AUTHORS
VINE DeLORIA JR./CLIFFORD LYTLE

PUBLISHER
PANTHEON BOOKS

Cover illustration for *The Nations Within*,
published Fall 1984.

Acrylic

200 ARTIST
JOSEPH CIARDIELLO

ART DIRECTOR
RICHARD BERENSON

PUBLISHER
READER'S DIGEST BOOKS

Illustration for Mark Twain's *A Connecticut Yankee in King Arthur's Court*, published 1984.

Pen and ink and watercolor

201 ARTIST/DESIGNER
JAMES McMULLAN

ART DIRECTOR
NANCY ETHEREDGE

AUTHOR
JORGE LUIS BORGES

PUBLISHER
E.P. DUTTON

Cover illustration for *Evaristo Carriego*,
published March 1984.

Watercolor on paper

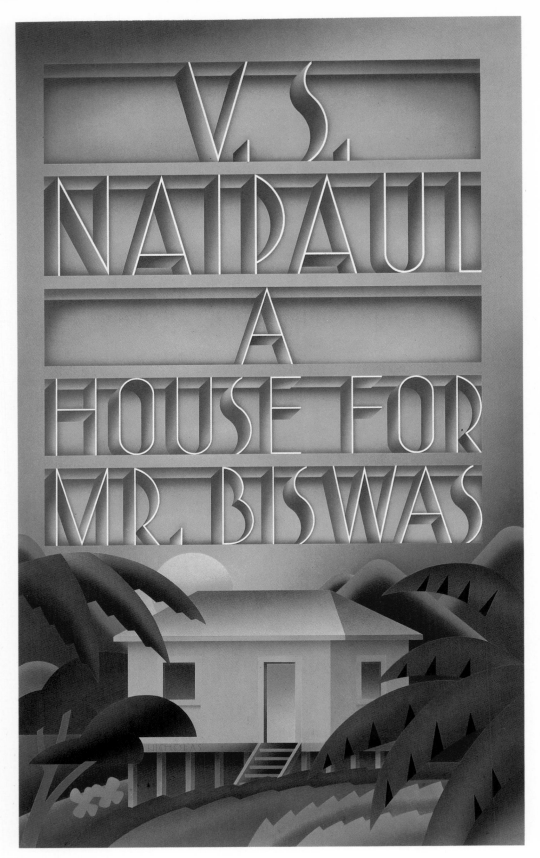

202 ARTIST
NICHOLAS GAETANO

ART DIRECTOR
JUDITH LOESER

AUTHOR
V.S. NAIPAUL

PUBLISHER
VINTAGE

Cover illustration for *A House for Mr. Biswas.*

Gouache

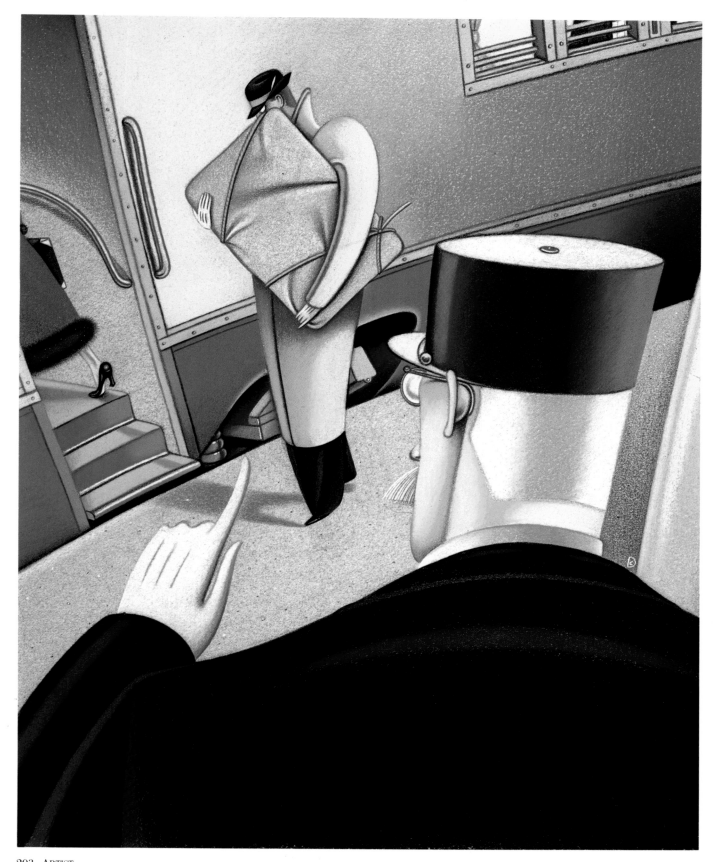

203 ARTIST
DAVE CALVER

DESIGNER/ART DIRECTOR
LOUISE FILI

AUTHOR
MARTIN PAGE

PUBLISHER
PANTHEON BOOKS

Cover illustration for *The Man Who Stole the
Mona Lisa*, published September 1984.

Colored pencil

204 ARTIST
NANCY STAHL

DESIGNER/ART DIRECTOR
WENDY BASS

EDITORS
A.M. ROSENTHAL/ARTHUR GELB

PUBLISHER
VILLARD BOOKS

Cover illustration for *The Sophisticated Traveler: Winter, Love It or Leave It,* published October 1984.

Gouache

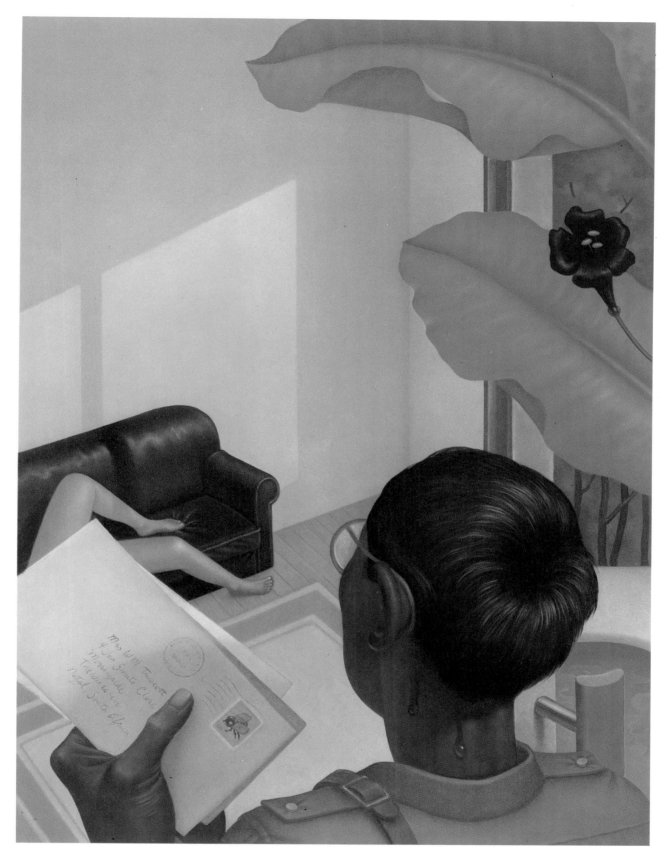

205 ARTIST
ROBERT GOLDSTROM

DESIGNER/ART DIRECTOR
LOUISE FILI

AUTHOR
JAMES McCLURE

PUBLISHER
PANTHEON BOOKS

Cover illustration for *The Artful Egg*,
published February 1985.

Oil on canvas

206 ARTIST
DAVID MONTIEL

ART DIRECTOR
JUDITH LOESER

AUTHOR
RING LARDNER

EDITOR
JOHN GLUSMAN

PUBLISHER
RANDOM HOUSE

Cover illustration for *You Know Me Al*,
published December 1984.

Acrylic paint

207 ARTIST/DESIGNER
MICHAEL MABRY

PUBLISHER
CITIZENS UTILITIES COMPANY OF CALIFORNIA

Directory cover for *Citizens Utilities Company of California*, published Summer 1984.

Paper cuts

208 ARTIST/DESIGNER
SEYMOUR CHWAST

AUTHORS
SEYMOUR CHWAST/PETER SCHICKELE

EDITOR
JIM FITZGERALD

PUBLISHER
DOUBLEDAY

Illustrations for *Happy Birthday, Bach,* published
March 1985.

Cello-tak and mixed media

212 ARTIST
LONNI SUE JOHNSON

DESIGNER
MILTON BATALION

ART DIRECTOR
GENE LIGHT

AUTHOR
MARTY ASHER

EDITOR
NANSEY NEIMAN

PUBLISHER
WARNER BOOKS

Cover and inside illustrations for *Fifty-Seven Reasons Not to Have a Nuclear War*, published Fall 1984.

Watercolor and ink

214 ARTIST
ROY WIEMANN

ART DIRECTOR
JOAN WILLENS

AUTHOR
CLEMENS BARTOLLAS

PUBLISHER
JOHN WILEY & SONS

Cover illustration for *Juvenile Delinquency*,
published 1985.

Color xerox collage and airbrush

ADVERTISING

This section includes illustrations for advertising in consumer,
trade, and professional magazines.

216 ARTIST
PAMELA H. PATRICK

ART DIRECTOR
JACK TAYLOR

COPYWRITER
HANK INMAN

ADVERTISING AGENCY
GRAY & ROGERS

CLIENT
SCIENCE 85 MAGAZINE

Illustration for a magazine advertisement with
copyline "Gulliver Among the Scientists."

Pastel

217 ARTIST
JAMES TUGHAN

ART DIRECTOR
HERMAN DYAL

COPYWRITER
SHERRY WAGNER

ADVERTISING AGENCY
BAUENCORP

CLIENT
SOUTHPORT DEVELOPMENTS

Advertisement for a luxury condominium
appearing in several magazines,
August 1984.

Chalk pastel

218 ARTIST
GUY BILLOUT

ART DIRECTOR
LARNEY WALKER

COPYWRITER
DENNIS GILLESPIE

ADVERTISING AGENCY
BBDM/CUNNINGHAM & WALSH

CLIENT
SIGNODE

Advertisement for a packaging firm with
copyline "How to Build a Winning Team"
appearing in *Business Week*, February 1985.

Watercolor

219 ARTIST
SEYMOUR CHWAST
ADVERTISING AGENCY
PAUL SHIELDS, DOREMUS & CO.
CLIENT
FORBES MAGAZINE

Advertisement for *Forbes Magazine*.

Cello-tak and rapidograph

220 ARTIST
ROBERT GIUSTI

ART DIRECTOR
LARRY G. WRIGHT

ADVERTISING AGENCY
UHLAN-WRIGHT

CLIENT
CAE SYSTEMS, INC.

Advertisement for design hardware with
copyline "We Understand the Fear of Losing
Your Design Investment" appearing in trade
magazines, 1984.

Acrylic on canvas

221   ARTIST
GARY MEYER

ART DIRECTOR
JOHN SINER

COPYWRITER
SARA WOOD

ADVERTISING AGENCY
TYCER FULTZ BELLACK

CLIENT
WESTERN MICROTECHNOLOGY

Advertisement for electronic systems with
copyline "The Outlook on High Technology
Has Never Been Greater" appearing in
Electronic News, May 21, 1984.

Gouache

POSTERS

This section includes poster illustrations for consumer products, magazines, institutions, and special events.

225 ARTIST
SEYMOUR CHWAST

ART DIRECTOR
DICK DAVIS

COPYWRITER
RICH BINELL

ADVERTISING AGENCY
ALTMAN AND MANLEY

CLIENT
MICROCOM, INC.

Poster for Microcom Modems with copyline
"Find the Seventeen Mistakes in This
Picture," February 1985.

PMS offset color printing

226 ARTIST/ART DIRECTOR
GARY KELLEY

CLIENT
ART DIRECTORS CLUB OF CINCINNATI

Poster promoting the artist's lecture and slide
presentation, September 1984.

Pastel

227 ARTIST
GARY KELLEY

ART DIRECTOR
DENIS HAGEN

COPYWRITER
JACK SEIPPS

ADVERTISING AGENCY
BOZELL-JACOBS ADVERTISING

CLIENT
ILLINOIS STATE LOTTERY

Poster advertising the Illinois Cashbox Instant
Lottery, February 1985.

Pastel.

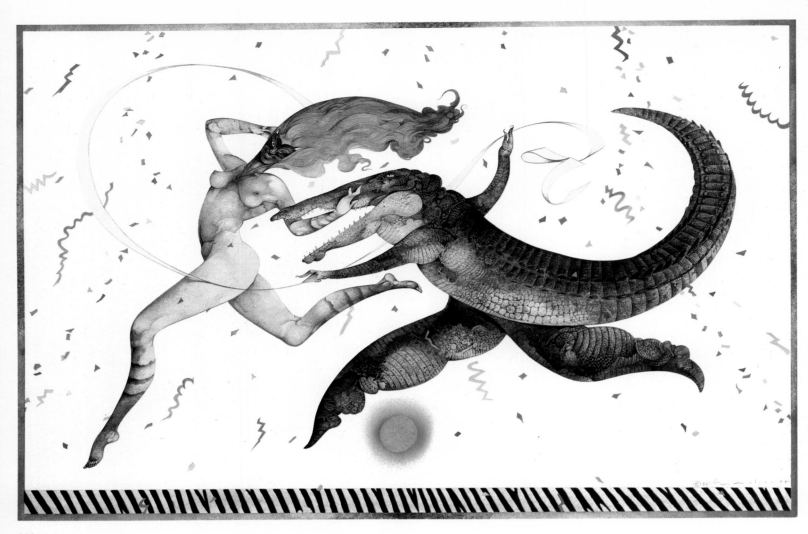

228 ARTIST
JAMES ENDICOTT

ART DIRECTOR
DAVID BARTELL

ADVERTISING AGENCY
DAVID BARTELL & ASSOCIATES

Poster sold during Mardi Gras.

Watercolor

229 ARTIST
HIDEAKI MORITA

ART DIRECTOR
YOSH KASHIWABARA

CLIENT
ASICS TIGER CORP.

Poster advertising athletic shoes with copyline
"Tiger Territory," 1984.

Gouache

230 ARTIST
CURT DOTY

ART DIRECTOR
PHIL HAYS

ADVERTISING AGENCY
ART CENTER COLLEGE OF DESIGN

CLIENT
THE WORLD HUNGER PROJECT

Poster with the copyline "End Hunger,
Achieve the Achievable," June 1984.

Acrylic

231 ARTIST/COPYWRITER
GARY KELLEY

ART DIRECTOR
JIM BORCHERDT

ADVERTISING AGENCY
D'ARCY-McMANUS-MASIUS

CLIENT
ANHEUSER-BUSCH/MICHELOB

Poster promoting a music tour by popular
black artists, Summer 1984.

Pastel

232 ARTIST
MICHAEL SCHWAB

ART DIRECTOR
CAROLYN BRENNAN

ADVERTISING AGENCY
MICHAEL SCHWAB DESIGN

CLIENT
WILKES BASHFORD

Poster to promote a special showing of
clothing designs by Garrick Anderson, 1984.

Ink and cut paper

233 ARTIST
MICHAEL SCHWAB

ART DIRECTORS
RAY MAZUR/VERONIQUE VIENNE

ADVERTISING AGENCY
MICHAEL SCHWAB DESIGN

CLIENT
THE DOT PRINTER

Promotional poster for the Dot Printer, 1985.

Cut paper

234 ARTIST
JAMES McMULLAN

ART DIRECTOR
CAROL CARSON

CLIENT
SCHOLASTIC PUBLISHING

Supplemental poster for Scholastic's *Let's
Find Out Magazine* with copyline "Leigh's
Holiday Alphabet Game." December 1984.

Watercolor on paper

235 ARTIST/ART DIRECTOR
MILTON GLASER

CLIENT
ELAINE BENSON GALLERY

Poster for an exhibition for the benefit of the
Animal Rescue Fund of the Hamptons.
Watercolor and crayon

236 ARTIST
WARD SCHUMAKER

Self-promotional poster with copyline "Lotte
Lenya 1928," 1985.

Pencil

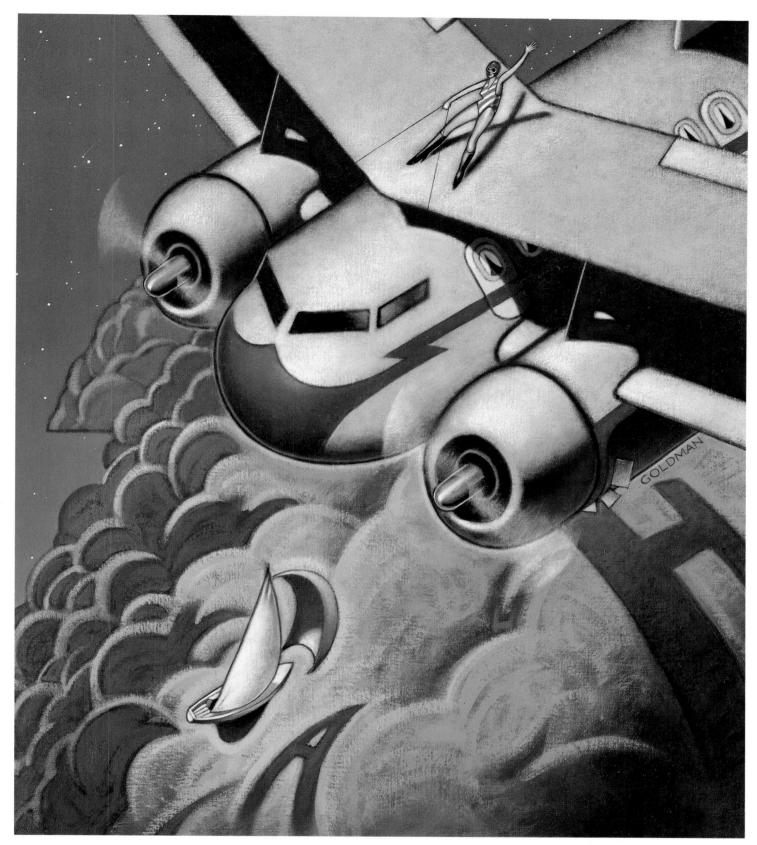

237 ARTIST
BART GOLDMAN

ART DIRECTOR
DON WELLER

ADVERTISING AGENCY
WELLER INSTITUTE FOR THE CURE OF DESIGN

CLIENT
ALPHA GRAPHIX

Poster advertising a type house with the
copyline "Dreamboat," March 1984.

Oil and acrylic

238 ARTIST
JOHN MARTIN

ART DIRECTOR
RICHARD CLEWES

COPYWRITER
BRUCE MacDONALD

ADVERTISING AGENCY
**MILLER MYERS BRUCE DALLA COSTA HARROD
MIRLIN**

CLIENT
THE STRATFORD FESTIVAL

Poster promoting the Stratford Festival's 1984
season, appearing mainly in Ontario and New
York, March-October 1984.

Acrylic

239 ARTIST
MALCOLM T. LIEPKE
ART DIRECTORS
MALCOLM T. LIEPKE/GRAHAM STILES
CLIENT
GREENWICH WORKSHOP GALLERIES

Poster advertising a gallery show.

Oil

240 ARTIST
BRALDT BRALDS

ART DIRECTOR
BOB BARRIE

COPYWRITER
PAT FALLON

ADVERTISING AGENCY
FALLON-McELLIGOTT-RICE

CLIENT
MINNESOTA ZOOLOGICAL GARDENS

Poster advertising the Minnesota zoo with
copyline "You Are the Missing Link. It Takes
More Than Animals to Make a Zoo Great,"
June/August 1984.

Oil on masonite panel

241 ARTIST
CURT DOTY

ART DIRECTOR
DAVID MOCARSKI

ADVERTISING AGENCY
NIELSEN & DAVID

CLIENT
METROPOLITAN MUSEUM OF ART

Poster announcing show at the museum with
copyline "A Retrospective of Amusement
Parks in America," 1985.

Acrylic and oil

242 ARTIST
PATRICK BLACKWELL

ART DIRECTOR
FRANK GLICKMAN

ADVERTISING AGENCY
FRANK GLICKMAN, INC.

Poster advertising the Museum of
Transportation displayed at a mall in
Massachusetts, August 1984.

India ink

PROMOTION

This section includes illustrations for calendars, greeting cards, brochures, record album covers, and self-promotion.

244 ARTIST/DESIGNER
LESLIE SZABO

ART DIRECTOR
CARA DEOUL

One in a series of portraits promoting French
designers for a fashion show, October 1984.

Pastel and colored pencil

245 ARTIST
ED LINDLOF

DESIGNER/ART DIRECTOR
SUZIE GILLOCK

CLIENT
REPUBLIC BANK REAL ESTATE BANKING GROUP

Historical map of San Antonio for a
promotional brochure.

Colored ink

246 ARTIST/DESIGNER
BRIAN ZICK

Self-promotional illustration.
Dye, acrylic, and ko-rec-type

247 ARTIST
BART GOLDMAN

ART DIRECTORS
BETSY RODDEN-LEE/CRAIG BUTLER

DESIGN GROUP
CRAIG BUTLER, INC.

Cover illustration for the L. A. Workbook
Directory, 1985.

Oil

ELWOOD H. SMITH
Self-promotional illustration.
Watercolor and India ink

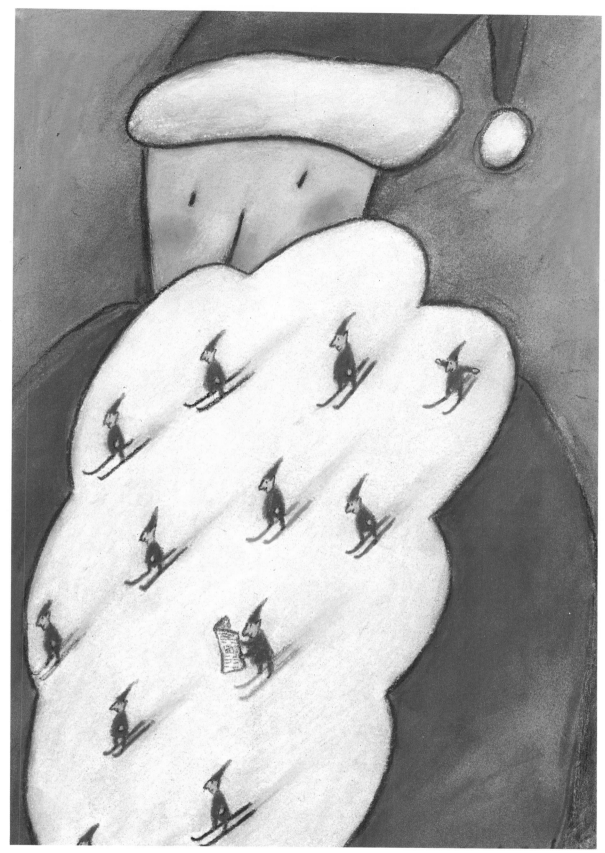

249 ARTIST/DESIGNER
BONNIE TIMMONS

ART DIRECTOR
TOM HOUGH

PUBLISHER
THE DENVER POST

Christmas card sent to advertisers, 1984.

Pastel

250 ARTIST
SANDRA HIGASHI

DESIGNER/ART DIRECTOR
MARTY NEUMEIER

DESIGN GROUP
NEUMEIER DESIGN TEAM

An open house invitation, February 1984.

Textured shading film assigned to 3 process
colors

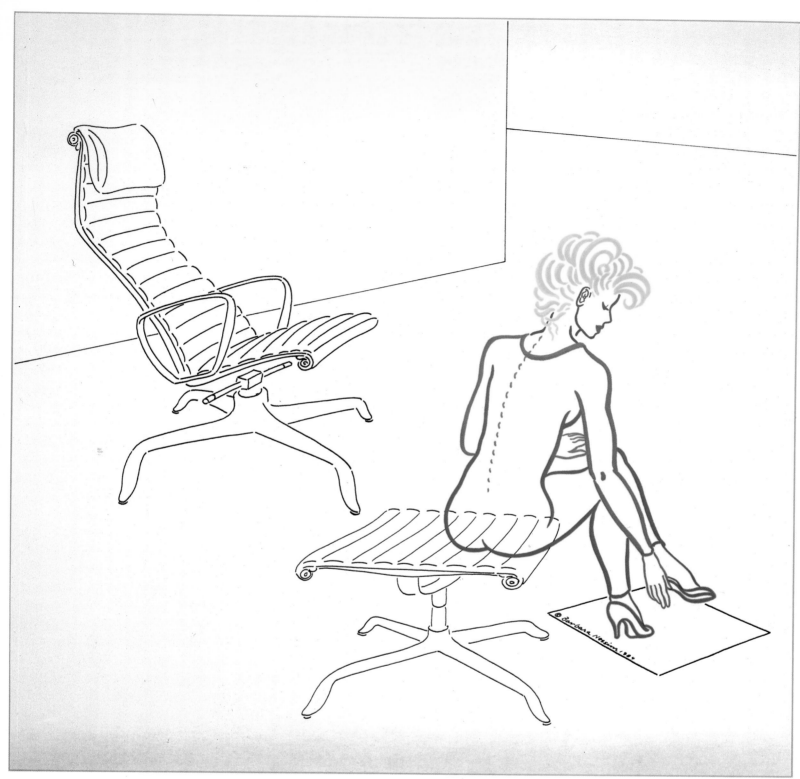

251 ARTIST
BARBARA NESSIM

DESIGNER/ART DIRECTOR
BARBARA LOVELAND

DESIGN GROUP
NESSIM & ASSOCIATES

PUBLISHER
HERMAN MILLER INC.

For a promotional brochure featuring artists'
interpretations of classic furniture, May 1984.

Gouache, pen and ink, and pastel

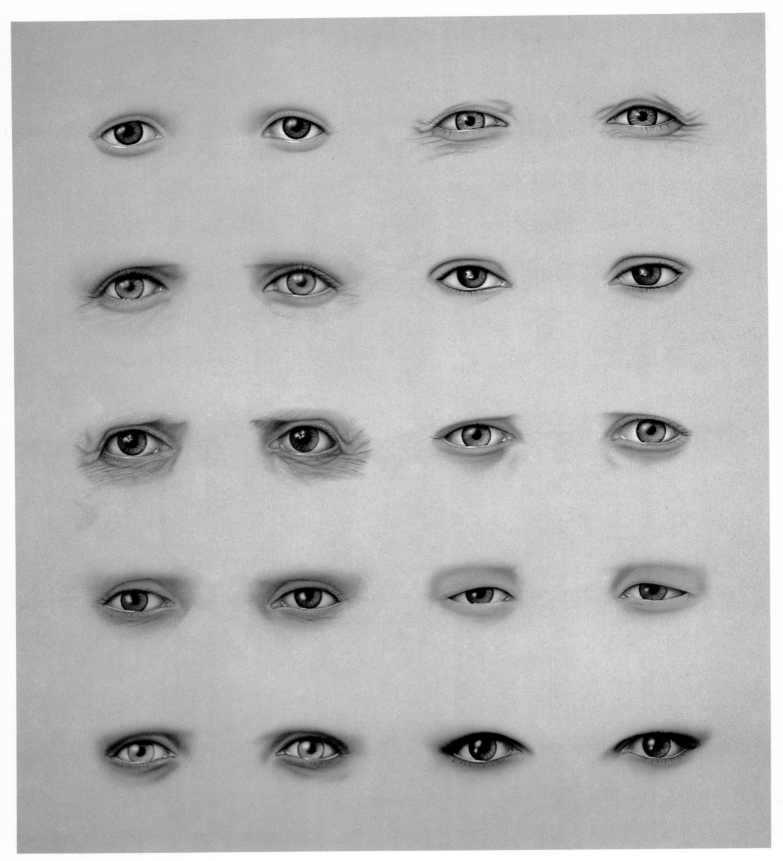

252 ARTIST
DAVID LOEW

DESIGNER/ART DIRECTOR
MICHAEL V. PHILLIPS

CLIENT
STEREO OPTICAL CO., INC.

Cover illustration for a sales aid introducing
new vision tester, October 1984.

Airbrush and pencil

253 ARTIST/DESIGNER
R.E. JORDAN

PUBLISHER
HALLMARK CARDS, INC.

Greeting card for Hallmark's 75th anniversary
collection.

Thermography

254 ARTIST/DESIGNER
LLYNNE BUSCHMAN
Self-promotional piece, September 1984.
Pastel

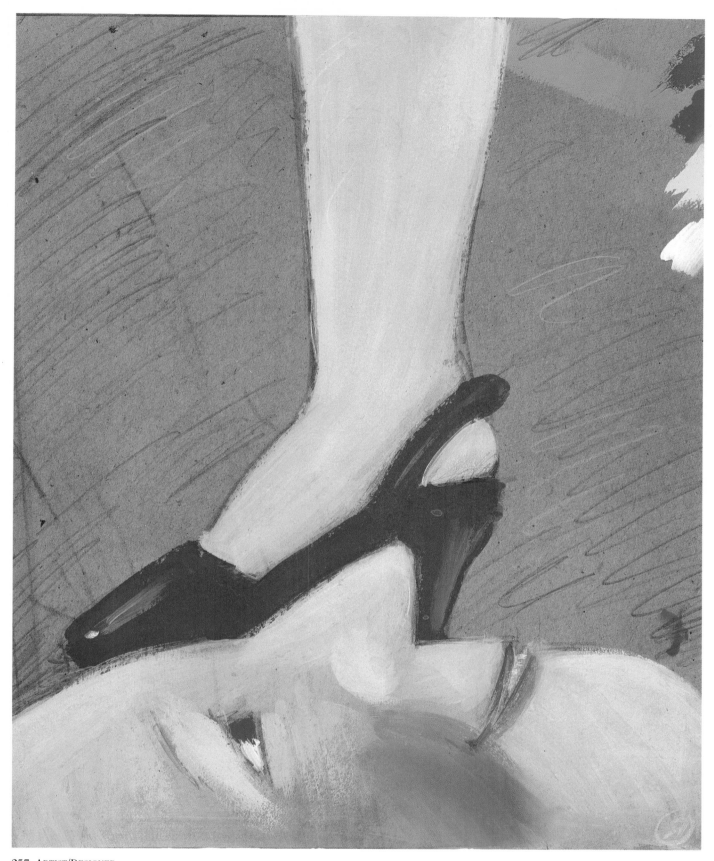

257 ARTIST/DESIGNER
RAFAL OLBINSKI
DESIGNER/GROUP/PUBLISHER
PAPERMANIA INT. STUDIO
Greeting card, Spring 1985.
Mixed media on board

258 ARTIST
MALCOLM T. LIEPKE

ART DIRECTOR
JAMES CRAIG

DESIGN GROUP
HALLWOOD DESIGN INC.

CLIENT
BENDER FABRICS

Two in a series of paintings for a promotional
brochure on the garment industry, May 1984.

Oil

260 ARTIST
SARA SCHWARTZ

DESIGNER/ART DIRECTOR
FRANK OLINSKY

DESIGN GROUP
MANHATTAN DESIGN

PUBLISHER
ZE RECORDS

Album cover for "John Cale Comes Alive,"
1984.

Colored pencil

261 ARTIST/DESIGNER
ANITA KUNZ

    Self-promotional Christmas card, 1984.

    Watercolor and gouache

262 ARTIST
WARREN GEBERT

One in a series of "household appliances"
used as a promotional mailer.

Housepaint and acrylic on rag paper

263 ARTIST/DESIGNER
JERRY CLEMENS

WRITER
JIM LANGDON

PUBLISHER
HALLMARK CARDS, INC.

Illustration for greeting card, February 1985.

Watercolor and prismacolor

264 ARTIST/DESIGNER
MAX PHILLIPS

PUBLISHER
POLLACK PRESS INC.

July page of a promotional desk calendar for a
printing company.

Collage, chalk pastel, and pencil

265 ARTIST
GARY KELLEY

DESIGNER
CHRIS HILL

ART DIRECTORS
SHINICHRO TORA/MITSUTOSHI HOSAKA

DESIGN GROUP
DAI NIPPON PRINTING CO., LTD.

PUBLISHER
HOTEL BARMEN'S ASSOCIATION

Illustration for a calendar distributed in
Japan, 1985.

Pastel

266 ARTIST
DOUG SMITH

DESIGNER/ART DIRECTOR
VICTOR LaPORTE

WRITER
VALJEAN McLENIGHAN

DESIGN GROUP
THE STURM COMMUNICATIONS GROUP, INC.

Brochure for the Christian Hospital Recovery
Center, October 1984.

Scratchboard

UNPUBLISHED WORK

This section includes commissioned but unpublished
illustrations, personal work produced by professionals, and the
work of students.

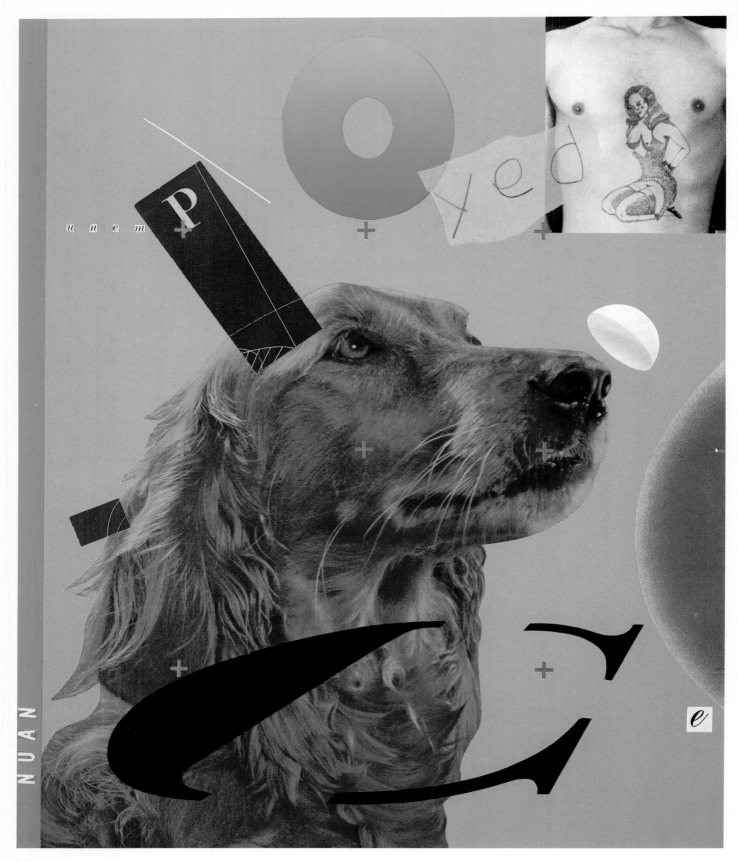

268 ARTIST
GENE GREIF
"Unemployed Nuance."
Collage

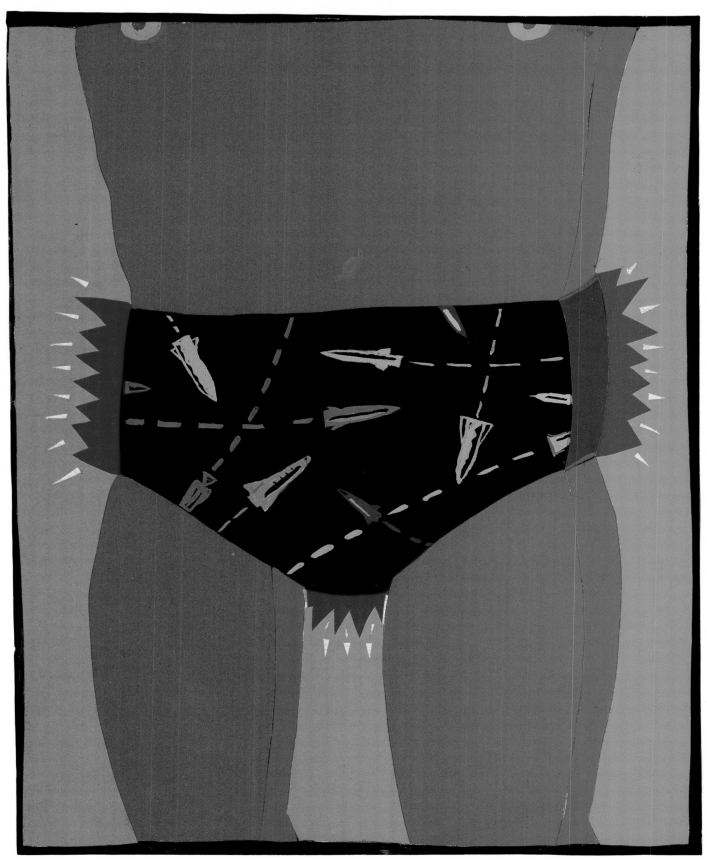

269 ARTIST
JOHN HERSEY
"Rocket Shorts."
Collage

270 ARTIST
ALISON SEIFFER

DESIGNER
SCOTT YARDLEY

For an unpublished book entitled *Uncle Wiggily Counting & Hopping and Hanging Around.*

Scratchboard

272 ARTIST
LANE SMITH
Personal work for ongoing "Animal Book."
Alkyd

273 ARTIST
DEBORAH HEALY
"Still Life With Fish."
Oil

274 ARTIST
BILL VUKSANOVICH

"After the Storm."
Oil

275 ARTIST
MICKEY PARASKEVAS
Portrait of Bob Geldorf.
Oil on canvas

276 ARTIST
BRENDA LEE TRACY

"Midnight."
  Dye, charcoal, and pastel

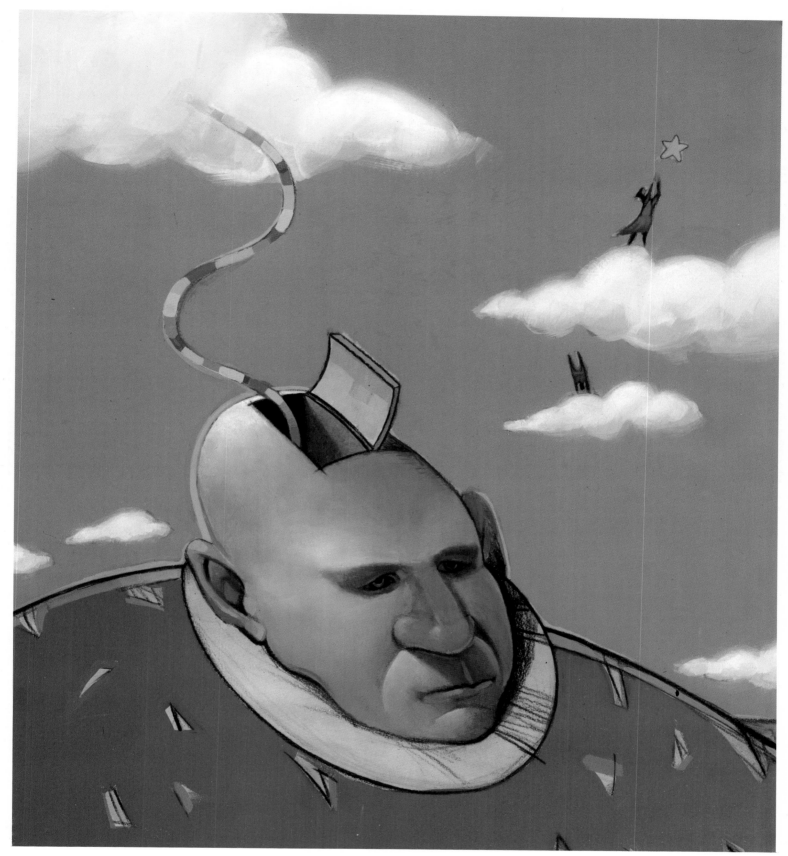

277 ARTIST
RAFAEL LOPEZ

"Man With Door in Head," a school
assignment for an HBO poster.
Watercolor and acrylic

278 ARTIST
COPIE

A student assignment on the homeless in New
York.
Mixed media

279 ARTIST
ELLEN KASKA
A student assignment on vigilantism.
Acrylic

280 ARTIST
ALISON SEIFFER

Drawing based on the story "Conversation
With a Supplicant" by Franz Kafka.

Mixed media on scratchboard

281 ARTIST
SALVADOR BRU

"Washington and the Obelisk," for a
promotional calendar commissioned by
Westland Printers.

Gouache and colored pencil

282 ARTIST
IRA M. KORMAN
Untitled.
Pastel

283 ARTIST
IRA M. KORMAN
"Sandy's Mother."
Charcoal

284 ARTIST
CHRISTINE WALKER
"Hanauma Bay."
Oil on canvas

285 ARTIST
KATHY TODD

"The Conversation."
Egg tempera and gouache on board

ROBERT NEUBECKER

Illustration for an article entitled "Fear of
Flying" commissioned by *Discover Magazine*.

Mixed media

287 ARTIST
PAUL WOLF

"Cowboy Chickens."
Pastel

ARTIST
ROGER CHOUINARD

Illustrations for an unpublished children's
book entitled *Amazing Animal Alphabet*.

Watercolor and gouache

290 ARTIST
LINDEN WILSON
"Bicycle Accident."
Oil pastel

291 ARTIST
DAVID AYRISS
Untitled.
Oil

292 ARTIST
MARK S. FISHER

"There is a Mountain," illustrating the lyrics
of Donovan.
Ink and watercolor

293 Artist
MARK S. FISHER

"Neutron," illustrating the lyrics of Donovan.
Xerox and watercolor

294 ARTIST
MARK S. FISHER

"Mad John's Escape," illustrating the lyrics of
Donovan.

Ink and watercolor

295 ARTIST
SARA SWAN

"Three Dalmations."

Pastel

296 ARTIST
NINA BERKSON

"Suburban Gothic."
Oil on paper

297 ARTIST
ROGER T. DE MUTH

"Waiter, there's a hare in my soup," one in a
series of illustrated puns.

Ink and cel-vinyl paint

298 ARTIST
MICHAEL McGURL
"Better Than Pennies."
Gouache

299   ARTIST
BARRY ROOT
"Man Juggling Piglets."
Watercolor and gouache

300 ARTIST
MARK H. ADAMS

"Flying or Falling, Manic Depression."
Gouache

301 ARTIST
MARK H. ADAMS
"Chez Chic."
Gouache

302 ARTIST
CATY BARTHOLOMEW
Untitled.
Acrylic

303 ARTIST
CATY BARTHOLOMEW
Untitled.
Acrylic

304 ARTIST
LILLA ROGERS
"A Bracing Option."
Charcoal, watercolor, and pastel

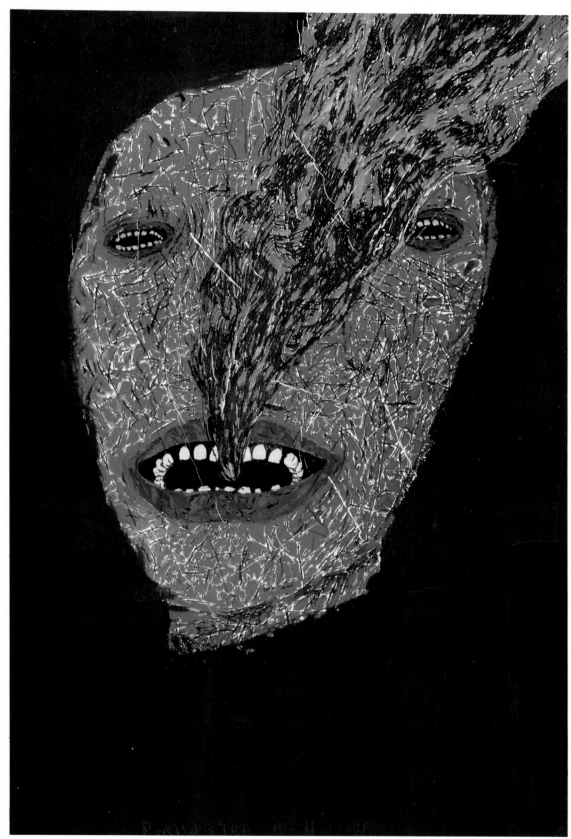

305 ARTIST
HENRIK DRESCHER
"Appetite."
Watercolor, ink, and varnish

306 ARTIST
GAY W. HOLLAND

Two in a series of illustrations for a children's
book entitled *The Scaredy Cat*. A school
assignment.

Colored pencil

308 ARTIST
BARBARA SAMUELS
"Domestic Life."
Watercolor and ink

309 ARTIST
POL TURGEON

"Room in Time," illustrating the John Collier
story "Are You Too Late or Was I Too Early."

Colored pencil

310 ARTIST
JAMES McMULLAN

Portrait of Philip Glass commissioned by *Time* magazine.

Watercolor on paper

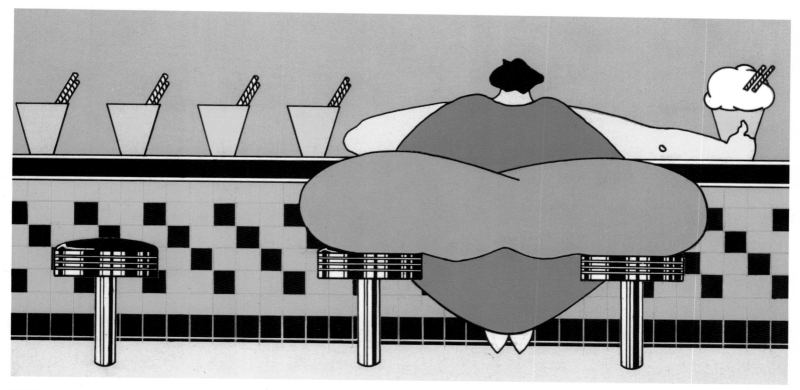

311 ARTIST
MORGAN PICKARD

Illustration for an article on obesity
commissioned by *Shape Magazine*.

Acrylic and ink

312 ARTIST
JOHN H. HOWARD
"Interiore Suspicioso."
Acrylic

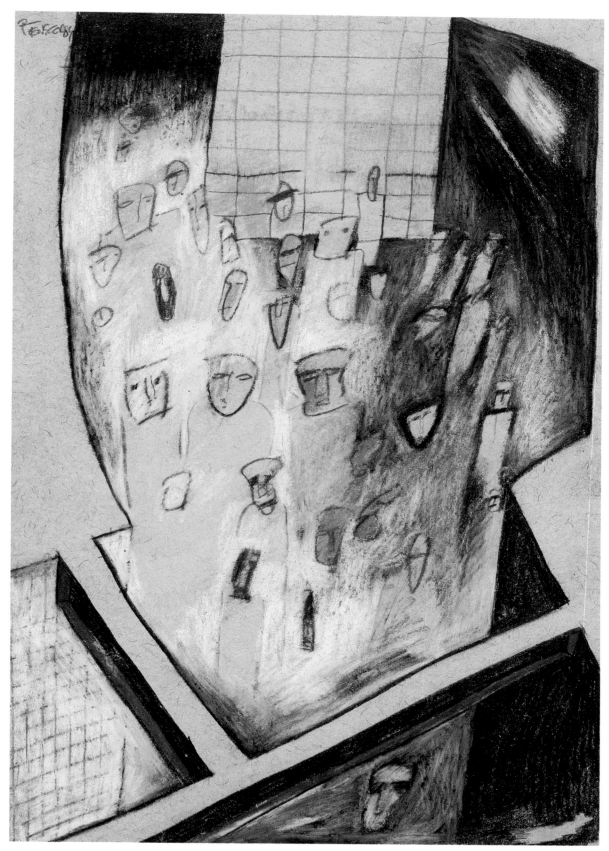

313 ARTIST
PETER TENGLER
"Transit."
Colored pencil on paper

FILM

This section includes film animation for advertising, television, and public service.

316 ANIMATORS
ED SMITH/TONY EASTMAN/PAUL SPARAGANO

ARTIST/DESIGNER
STEVEN GUARNACCIA

DIRECTOR
R.O. BLECHMAN

WRITER
DAN ALTMAN

ART DIRECTOR
BOB MANLEY

AGENCY
ALTMAN & MANLEY

PRODUCTION COMPANY
THE INK TANK

CLIENT
MULTIGROUP HOUSE PLAN

Advertising commercial entitled "Multigroup."

60 seconds

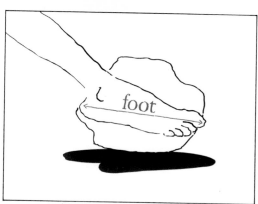

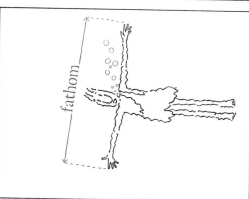

317 ANIMATOR
ED SMITH

ARTIST/DIRECTOR
R.O. BLECHMAN

WRITER/PRODUCER
FRANKLIN GETCHALL

PRODUCTION COMPANY
THE INK TANK

CLIENT
CHILDREN'S TELEVISION WORKSHOP

Animated segment to instruct children on
units of measurement entitled "A Foot is a
Foot."

5 minutes

318 ANIMATOR
GARY MOONEY

DESIGNER/DIRECTOR
BOB KURTZ

WRITER
MARK ELLIS

ART DIRECTOR
LORING GROVE

AGENCY PRODUCER
JOANNE GUARDIANI

AGENCY
WEIGHTMAN ADVERTISING, INC.

PRODUCTION COMPANY
KURTZ & FRIENDS

CLIENT
ALPO PETFOODS

Advertising commercial entitled "Million Dollar Promo."

30 seconds

319 ANIMATORS
JEFF JURICH/JAMES WAHLBERG

ARTIST
BONNIE TIMMONS

DIRECTOR
JAMES WAHLBERG

ART DIRECTOR
TODD BALLARD

PRODUCER
ELIZABETH MOORE

AGENCY
BROYLES, ALLEBAUGH AND DAVIS

PRODUCTION COMPANY
CELLULOID STUDIOS

CLIENT
CITY OF DENVER

"Celebrate 125," a public service spot for
Denver's 125th anniversary festivities.

30 minutes

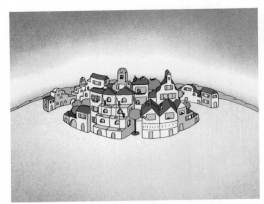

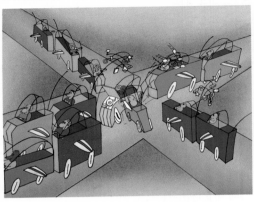

320 ANIMATORS/DESIGNERS
HOWARD DANELOWITZ/TRACY KIRSHENBAUM

DIRECTOR/ART DIRECTOR
HOWARD DANELOWITZ

PRODUCTION COMPANY
NEW YORK ANIMATION

CLIENT
HBO

Animated film entitled "Oddityville" for an
HBO program "Brain Games."

3:30 minutes

INDEX

Names and addresses of contributing artists. Index of designers, art directors, publications, publishers, design groups, advertising agencies, copywriters, film directors, production companies, and clients.

AMERICAN ILLUSTRATION®

Every fall American Illustration, Inc. has a Graphic
Arts Weekend symposium on creativity which attracts
people from all over the world. It is held in New York
and features "Studio Visits" whereby students and
professionals in the graphic arts field visit with illustrators, film animators, art directors, and designers in
their studios.

If you would like to know more about this and other
American Illustration® activities, or if you are a practicing illustrator, artist, or student and want to submit
work to the annual competition, write to:

American Illustration, Inc.
67 Irving Place
New York, New York 10003
(212) 460-5558

Edward Booth-Clibborn
President

THE COMMITTEE

Julian Allen
Illustrator, New York

Carol Carson
Freelance Graphic Designer, New York

Seymour Chwast
Director, Pushpin Lubalin Peckolick
New York

Steven Heller
Art Director, *New York*
Times Book Review, New York

Doug Johnson
Designer & Illustrator
Performing Dogs Advertising, New York

Louise Kollenbaum
Art Director, *Mother Jones*
San Francisco

John Macfarlane
Publisher, *Saturday Night*, Toronto

James McMullan
Designer & Illustrator
Visible Studio Inc., New York

Robert Priest
Art Director, *Us*, New York